"You will never need to buy another book on knots."
—*Pittsburgh Tribune-Review*

"An excellent resource for beginning and intermediate backcountry adventurers."
—*Outside Bozeman*

"Outdoorsy folk have been known to be obsessive about certain things, and this book could no doubt serve as a quintessential reference book."
—*Reno Gazette-Journal*

"The *Outdoor Knots Book* is a great resource for any outdoor types in your family. This concise and well-illustrated book details how to make more than 40 of the most common (and not so common) rope knots that are used by campers, hikers, paddlers and climbers."
—*Camping Life magazine*

"This book is not to be missed if you're an outdoors person....The scope of the book makes it a must-read for outdoors enthusiasts.... The how-to-tie instructions and photographs will soon have you making a double bowline with out a hitch."
—*Los Angeles Daily News*

"A thorough guide."
—*Sacramento Bee*

"Whether cinching down a load on a horse or a pickup, securing a tent or a canopy, this book has some tried-and-true traditional and relatively new knots."
—*Salem Statesman Journal*

"The preferred alternative for someone who wants a handy, practical reference."
—*Great Falls Tribune*

mountaineers
outdoor
basics

The Outdoor Knots Book

Hikers | **Campers**

Climbers | **Kayakers**

Clyde Soles

THE MOUNTAINEERS BOOKS

THE MOUNTAINEERS BOOKS
is the nonprofit publishing arm of The Mountaineers Club,
an organization founded in 1906 and dedicated to the exploration,
preservation, and enjoyment of outdoor and wilderness areas.

1001 SW Klickitat Way, Suite 201, Seattle, WA 98134

Text and photographs © 2004 by Clyde Soles

First printing 2004, second printing 2005

Published simultaneously in Great Britain by Cordee, 3a DeMontfort Street, Leicester, England, LE1 7HD

Manufactured in the United States of America

Acquiring Editor: Cassandra Conyers
Project Editor: Kate Rogers
Copy Editor: Joan Gregory
Cover Design: Karen Schober
Interior Design: The Mountaineers Books
Layout Artist: Ani Rucki

Cover photograph: © Jim Martin

Library of Congress Cataloging-in-Publication Data
Soles, Clyde, 1959-
  The outdoor knots book / Clyde Soles.— 1st ed.
    p. cm.
Includes bibliographical references and index.
  ISBN 0-89886-962-5 (pbk.)
  1. Climbing knots. 2. Outdoor life. I. Title.
  GV200.19.K56S65 2004
  796.52'2—dc22
                            2003025508

Contents

Foreword

Like many of you, I managed to get along in the outdoors for years knowing only a handful of knots. I adhered to the common wisdom that there was no need for all "them fancy knots" and muddled through with my basic set—sometimes with surprising, and unpleasant, results.

Eventually, I started picking up knot and rope-handling tricks that greatly simplified life when I was playing in the mountains and on rivers. Adding to my repertoire enhanced both my speed and safety. There is much to be said for quickly tying the appropriate knot instead of dinking around trying to make something work.

Numerous books have been written about knots. Most overwhelm readers with fifty ways of joining two ropes or a hundred variations of a loop, with hardly any discussion of why one knot might be better than another. The preponderance of nautical knots that have few if any applications for nonsailors (or even real sailors) dilutes the usefulness of many knot books. And surprisingly, very few give much information about the ropes themselves.

In *The Outdoor Knots Book*, I have narrowed the list of knots down to those most practical for hikers, campers, climbers, scramblers, canoeists, kayakers, and pretty much anyone else who spends time playing outside. Some you probably already know, though I might teach you new tying methods or helpful variations. Others may be knots you were aware of but too intimidated to try, or perhaps you were unclear about their applications and advantages. Yet others may be completely new additions to your bag of tricks.

Perhaps I've left out your favorite knot—there are certainly many other worthy candidates. Use these described here to build your knowledge base, then supplement with additional knots as the need arises.

Since knots depend on ropes and webbing, I've devoted the first couple chapters to describing the various materials and processes used in making cordage. Armed with this knowledge, you can select the best rope or webbing for the job. Equally important is learning how to care for cordage and tricks for handling ropes to avoid snafus.

After you have read the information on selecting and caring for cordage, the best way to use *The Outdoor Knots Book* is to sit down with rope in hand. A forgotten knot does you no good. Read the words, study the pictures, and *practice* each knot. When you can tie it with your eyes closed, you will have really learned a knot.

Warning: Different ropes, or combinations of ropes, can yield very different results when knotted. When reliability is critical to safety, be certain to test the specific ropes and knots beforehand.

Acknowledgments

Over the years, many people have contributed to my knowledge of ropes and knots. When I was the Gear Editor at *Rock & Ice* magazine, I wrote several reviews of climbing ropes, visited five rope manufacturers in the United States and Europe to watch production, talked with designers, and performed tests. This experience gave me a greater appreciation for ropes as well as a better understanding of their limitations.

A major contributor to this work has been Dan Lehman, a knot aficionado, who provided excellent commentary. Thanks to Michelle Harris who kindly demonstrated coiling techniques. Others who have helped out, knowingly or not, include Chris Harmston, Karl Lew, Loui McCurley, and Regan Velasquez. Also, thanks again to my dad, who started me in the outdoors when I was six.

Chapter
1

Rope Materials & Construction

Ropes seem mundane at first. But they are pretty cool when you take a closer look. A rope is one of mankind's oldest tools and a good example of synergy: The whole is greater than the sum of its parts. Without rope, neither Stonehenge nor the Great Pyramids nor many other ancient wonders would have been possible.

Ropes did not change much for, oh, say 50,000 years. Probably much longer. Once we progressed beyond vines, it was always a matter of twisting some natural fibers—plant stalks, tree bark, hair, sinew, whatever—into cohesive units. Refinements were made, but the basics were worked out long ago.

Then came synthetics. And improved manufacturing processes. In the 1940s, the new materials replaced natural fibers in countless applications and revolutionized the world. In the 1970s, rope-making technology took another leap forward with new construction technologies and combinations of materials. Then in the 1980s, hyper-strong fibers emerged and ropes previously considered impossible became available. It is possible that another revolution in rope technology is around the corner.

ROPE & WEBBING MATERIALS

Whether it is 2-millimeter parachute cord or 240-mm off-shore mooring line, most ropes and webbing are made from a handful of materials. Like the ingredients in a recipe, the raw materials determine the basic properties of the final product. And good cooks know that both the quality of the ingredients and how you combine them are vital to creating a tasty meal.

An understanding of the basic properties of the materials used in ropes and webbing is important for good purchasing decisions. No less important are using and caring for the cordage properly, to ensure optimal performance and safety.

While the raw stuff of cordage (such as nylon and polyester) is essentially the same from rope to rope, manufacturers can tweak the fibers during production. How the molten material is stretched and cooled can change the performance of the final product. "Tensilizing" the fibers (causing the molecules to align) increases strength. Manufacturers can add dyes to the molten material or dye the fibers afterward. The former process tends to be cheaper but results in a weaker product. Various finishes can be applied to provide lubrication, both for smoother running through machines during rope construction and for a softer hand, and some of these coatings last longer than others. Fibers can also be finished to increase ultraviolet (UV) protection, water repellency, and/or abrasion resistance.

While this minutia is too complex for end-users to fret about, it helps explain why some ropes that cost less than others don't look or feel any different—at first. Producing an inexpensive rope generally means cutting costs at every step and, while the resulting ropes are safe when used correctly, they often don't perform as well in the long run.

Natural

Although much about the history of rope making has been lost in antiquity, cave paintings in Spain dating to 17,000 B.C. depict ropes in use, and a rope fishing net found in Finland is about 9,000 years old. Until 1942, humans relied upon natural fibers such as hemp, manila, and sinew (the latter can be as strong as nylon) for rope making. Many natural fibers are still used today by the industrial world and indeed retain some advantages over synthetic materials.

Natural fiber ropes tend to be inexpensive, are surprisingly abrasion resistant, can withstand prolonged exposure to sunlight without loss of strength, and have a high tolerance for heat. These qualities make natural fiber ropes ideal for utilitarian purposes such as lashing poles together, particularly if the entire structure is intended to be biodegradable.

Among the most common natural fiber used in ropes is manila, which comes from the stalks of the abaca, a relative of the banana plant that is found in the Philippines (hence the name) as well as in Ecuador. Low-grade manila ropes tend to be coarse and stiff, so they are rough on the hands, while higher grades are smooth and supple. Manila ropes are nearly as strong as polypropylene ropes and actually get stronger when wet. Sometimes called manila hemp, the ropes are golden brown to nearly white (the latter are better). In 1864, the British Alpine Club determined that 10-mm manila hemp, which weighed about 75 grams per meter (g/m), was the best choice for climbing, and the "Alpine Club rope" became the standard for the remainder of the century.

A similar fiber comes from sisal, a desert plant in the agave family (think yuccas and tequila). Ropes made from sisal are not as smooth as those made from manila, and they are about 20 percent weaker. Sisal is used for making a cheap utility rope and is also popular for cat-scratching posts. Sisal ropes are generally off-white in color (green if treated to resist rotting).

For thousands of years in sailing, hemp from cannibis was the material of choice for making ropes. It is among the strongest of the natural fibers and can be used to produce ropes with good handling as well as sturdy fabrics for sails ("canvas" comes from the ancient Greek *kannabis*). However, hemp had to be tarred to survive in seawater, so the maritime world largely switched to manila around 1830. Industrial hemp contains less than 1 percent THC, the active ingredient in marijuana, so the value is in the stalks. When the Philippines were under Japanese control during World War II, the U.S. government encouraged the growing of hemp (the production goal in 1943 was 300,000 acres). Italian hemp was the material of choice for climbing ropes until synthetics came along. Today, hemp ropes, which are light tan, are too expensive for utility purposes.

Many other plant products are still used for making ropes, including coir (from coconut husks), flax, jute, and cotton. For the most part, these are softer yet weaker than the other natural fibers; their main advantages are low price and regional availability. Coir ropes are the only natural fiber ropes that float and resist seawater damage.

Polyamide (Nylon)

Compared to plant fibers, nylon is significantly stronger and impervious to rot and mildew damage. Of particular importance to climbers (and a source of frustration for sailors), nylon stretches a great deal under load. This elongation helps absorb the energy of a fall instead of transmitting it to climbers and their protection (nuts, cams, and other anchors).

On February 28, 1935, a team of researchers at DuPont, led by Wallace Carothers, introduced the material we now call nylon, the second synthetic fiber (rayon was first, in 1889). Originally used for toothbrush bristles, nylon became wildly successful as a replacement for silk in leg stockings (though less comfortable, it was more durable). During World War II, the first nylon ropes were built and soon became the top choice for many applications.

What Carothers and his team created was a macromolecule (polymer) containing many amide groups joined in a row—a polyamide. The number of carbon atoms in sections of the new molecule gives it the designation Type 6,6 (often seen without a comma or with a period or slash between the numbers). Lacking a name for this new synthetic material, a committee selected the word "nylon" (a spin-off of "no-run") from a list of 300 candidates. Though DuPont patented the molecule, they elected to allow the name to become generic, and nylon became a household word.

During the prelude to war, the German company I. G. Farben (now Bayer) was also working on synthetic fibers. Though Carothers had ruled out the possibility, Paul Schlack managed to synthesize polyamide Type 6 with properties very similar to nylon. Originally marketed as "perlon," it is now called nylon 6. Many other versions of nylon have also been developed, such as 6,12 and even a 66,6 blend, but they are not used in ropes.

For many applications, the differences between nylon 6 and nylon 66 are insignificant. However, the structure of nylon 6 gives it greater tenacity, elongation, and flexibility—all desirable properties in dynamic climbing ropes. Nylon 66, on the other hand, has a somewhat higher melting point. This, along with less stretch, is better for static ropes used in caving and rescue applications.

Nylon has good resistance to degradation by ultraviolet (UV) rays in sunlight. Tests of slightly faded climbing ropes and webbing have shown minimal strength loss, in part because the thickness protects the inner material. However, nylon does degrade after long exposure to the elements; the degree to which this happens depends on dyes (white and black are the most resistent) and other variables. Climbers should, therefore, replace old nylon rappel anchors that are bleached white and crunchy, rather than risk a life.

A major concern with nylon is that strong mineral acids (such as sulfuric, nitric, and hydrochloric acid) can decompose the fibers without visible effects. Thus it is very important to store nylon cordage well away from possible contamination, even from fumes. This includes avoiding storage in automobile trunks with nonsealed car batteries. Strong bleach can also weaken nylon, though a weak solution may be used to disinfect ropes contaminated with blood.

Fortunately, nylon is relatively impervious to alkalis and organic solvents. The active ingredient in insect repellents (DEET) and even in gasoline have no effect. But nobody can be certain about all the other chemicals that may be found in solvents, so it is wise to avoid any chemical contamination of nylon life lines.

Properly stored nylon does not lose strength with age, so there is little concern that old ropes will break in normal conditions. However, the shock-absorbing ability of nylon does decrease with time, which will subject gear and/or a falling climber to greater forces than normal. More significant, older nylon ropes have less resistance to cutting over an edge during a fall.

Compared to other synthetic fibers, nylon absorbs a great deal of water—up to 8 percent of its weight for nylon 66 and 9.5 percent for nylon 6 at saturation. This water swells the nylon molecule, which reduces strength by as much as 25 percent (10 to 12 percent is more typical) and significantly decreases abrasion resistance. Testing of wet dynamic climbing ropes yields the same results as those of a dry rope heated to about 160°F (71°C). Thus all nylon ropes that are likely to get wet need a coating to slow water absorption. Neither fresh nor seawater will harm nylon, and it regains its strength upon drying; rinse seawater off to remove salts.

Polyester (Dacron, Terylene)

A few years after nylon was invented, two British chemists expanded upon Carother's research. In 1941 they patented polyethylene terephthalate (PET), which is now the most common form of polyester, used in everything from plastic bottles to leisure suits. Imperial Chemical Industries marketed PET as Terylene and DuPont purchased the rights in 1945 and produced Dacron.

Ropes made from polyester fibers are particularly well suited to marine applications because they are about as strong as nylon ropes when dry and do not lose any strength when wet (polyester absorbs only 1 percent of its weight in water). Furthermore, polyester ropes exhibit low creep (static elongation), which means they don't stretch much when under a sustained load; this makes them good for rigging sailboats. Yet because they have moderate stretch (12 to 15 percent) at the breaking point, they can tolerate a sudden shock load. It is also more resistant to attack by acids and organic solvents, making polyester ropes good for industrial applications.

Other advantages of polyester over most other synthetics are superior resistance to UV degradation and abrasion. Therefore, polyester is often combined with polypropylene in ropes used by arborists and mariners.

Polyester is also commonly used in static ropes for climbing and caving. Often the outer sheath is polyester with an inner core of nylon; the cost of the raw materials is about the same. One drawback to polyester from the climber's viewpoint is that the ropes tend to be somewhat heavy due to polyester's high specific gravity (1.38 versus 1.14 for nylon).

Polypropylene

Discovered by two Italian chemists in 1954 (one of whom, Guilio Natta, would share a Nobel prize for his research), polypropylene (PP) is used to produce a wide range of ropes. The material is inexpensive to manufacture from petroleum or natural gas and is nearly inert to all chemicals, which makes it especially useful for commercial and industrial applications. Fibers are produced either by extrusion of a sheet of film that is then split with knives or extrusion of monofilaments.

One of polypropylene's primary advantages is a very low specific gravity (0.91), which makes it the lightest of rope-making materials. Polypro, as most people call it, is the most common material used for ropes that must float on water, such as river rescue ropes, tow lines for water skiing, and painters on boats (prevents fouling the propeller). Even when left in water for extended periods, polypropylene does not absorb any moisture or lose strength.

Polypro ropes are reasonably strong and generally the least expensive of synthetics, so they're used for a variety of utility purposes. However, they have a high degree of creep and are only moderately abrasion resistant. Typically, polypro ropes are very slick when new and have a rough, coarse feel after they have been used for a while.

Since polypro has a low melting point (330°F, 165°C) and loses nearly all its strength at a mere 200°F (93°C), it should never be used where a high amount of friction can be generated. Polypro also has a low temperature working limit of −20°F (−29°C), which may make it unsuitable for use in severe winter conditions.

Because they are cheap and lightweight, polypro ropes are often used on mountaineering expeditions where thousands of feet of line are fixed in place. These are adequate for protecting tricky sections on moderate terrain, but vertical work should be done on nylon or polyester static lines. Unless it has added stabilizers (carbon black is the most effective), polypro degrades fairly quickly in sunlight. Especially at high altitudes where UV rays are two to three times more intense than at sea level, old polypro ropes should never be trusted.

Polyethylene (HDPE)

Two scientists at Imperial Chemical Industries first synthesized polyethylene (PE) in 1934. The synthetic proved invaluable during the war, but it required a very expensive manufacturing process. The original polyethylene has a relatively low density with many side branches (LDPE) and is not suitable for ropes (though it is superb for films). In 1953, Karl Ziegler (who shared the Nobel with Natta) developed a catalyst that yielded a linear form of polyethylene with a much higher density (HDPE), and it was put into production two years later.

Both polyethylene and polypropylene are in a class of polymers called polyolefin (when polypro underwear fell out of favor, some companies who developed improved versions simply called it olefin to avoid the stigma). Not surprisingly, HDPE and polypro share many similar properties, including chemical inertness, negligible moisture absorption, the ability to float on water (specific gravity 0.95), and low cost. HDPE also does not hold up well to UV unless stabilizers have been added during production. Because of their slippery nature, polyolefin ropes often don't hold knots well.

Of major importance, HDPE has a very low melting point (only 285°F, 140°C) and upper working temperature (150°F, 65°C). This limitation precludes polyethylene ropes and webbing from many applications. On the other hand, the material stays flexible down to –100°F (–73°C), so mushers prefer it for rigging dog-sled harnesses.

Aramid (Kevlar, Twaron, Technora)

In 1964, Stephanie Kwolek, a researcher at DuPont, was assigned the task of developing new polymers that might replace steel in tires (a gas shortage was pending and the weight savings could reduce fuel consumption). In a moment of serendipity, she mixed a polymer and solvent and got an unexpected result—the first aramid (short for aromatic polyamide). Aramids revolutionized the fabric and cordage industries and opened up a field of science called liquid crystalline solutions.

While related to nylon, the golden fiber proved vastly stronger and more heat tolerant. Kevlar first appeared in 1975, when it was used in bulletproof vests. Its use has expanded to a wide array of products, and now over a half dozen types of the aramid are now available. Ropes made of Kevlar are about half the diameter and weight of conventional ropes yet equally as strong. Although aramids are fairly dense (specific gravity 1.44), they are so strong that less material is needed.

However, unlike nylon or polyester ropes, those made with aramids have very little stretch or ability to absorb shocks. To protect the structural core from UV light and abrasion, ropes made with aramids usually have an outer sheath of polyester.

The very linear molecular structure of Kevlar and Twaron (another type of aramid) makes them strong lengthwise but relatively weak laterally, resulting in poor abrasion resistance. Internal abrasion (termed "flex fatigue") means that these aramids wear out quickly when run over a pulley. They also lose significant strength when knotted, due to the tight bend radius. Because the sheath hides such damage from view, aramid core ropes can fail without warning—thus, they are no longer used in the outdoor recreation world.

A related product called Technora is an aramid co-polymer with stronger bonds between the linear chains, enabling it to hold up better to abrasion and flex fatigue. This characteristic makes it a better choice for use as accessory cord to sling-climbing protection and as a "cordelette" (a loop of rope used for belay anchors). A 5-mm cord with a Technora core and nylon or polyester sheath can equal the strength of 7-mm nylon cord. The narrower line reduces bulk and squeezes into tight constrictions in rock; however, the high-tech stuff also costs nearly three times more than nylon ropes.

High Modulus Polyethylene (HMPE) (Spectra, Dyneema)

A year after Kevlar came on the market, scientists at Dutch State Mines (DSM) developed a process for dissolving polyethylene to create a gel that can be spun and drawn to make fibers. The technique produces an ultrahigh-molecular-weight fiber with a high modulus (UHMWPE or HMPE), which basically means it is super strong and very light-weight—ten times stronger than steel for equal weight.

Origianlly sold as Dyneema in Europe and Spectra in the United States, and available in different grades, HMPE retains many of the good properties of normal polyethylene: light enough to float (specific gravity 0.97), unaffected by water, very resistant to chemicals. Plus, it is very abrasion resistant, holds up well against flex fatigue, and does not degrade in sunlight. However, HMPE also shares some of the drawbacks of polyethylene, including a slippery surface, minimal shock absorption, significant creep, and a low melting point (297°F, 147°C).

Accessory cord with an HMPE (or aramid) core needs to be tied with a triple fisherman's bend to ensure no slippage. Most webbing woven with HMPE does not hold knots well—they pull right through—so runners should be sewn. (A few HMPE/nylon webbings do hold knots, but their reliability depends upon the ratio and weave. Since these factors are not readily identifiable, err on the side of caution and use sewn runners.) In a dire emergency, it may be necessary to cut a sewn HMPE runner so it can be tied around an object (tree, piton eye, V-thread). In such a situation, cut right through the middle of the overlap so that the bulky ends form stoppers and use a double fisherman's bend.

Despite its limitations, HMPE is a superb material for climbing where low bulk, light weight, and high strength are important. For example, new generations of webbing are only 8 mm wide yet equally as strong and half the weight as nylon webbing that is 18 mm wide.

Exotic Materials (Vectran, Zylon, etc.)

In the marine and industrial worlds, where ropes are used to tow aircraft carriers and moor oil rigs to the ocean floor, they are huge money. This of course means serious competition for even stronger and lighter fibers. Quite a few materials even more exotic than aramids and HMPE have been developed and more are in the labs; some may eventually trickle down to the outdoor recreation world.

One material that has been tried and abandoned for high-strength accessory cord is liquid crystal polymer (Vectran), which takes gel spinning to the next level by using electricity to align molecules. While good in principle, and popular in the sailing world, Vectran-core cordelettes yielded disappointing test results, so Vectran is no longer sold for climbing purposes.

Other new technologies include PBO (poly-paraphenylene-2 6-benzobisoxazole), marketed as Zylon, which though stronger than HMPE does not hold up well to flexing and abrasion. A new type of polyester known as PEN (polyethylene naphthalate) and sold as Pentex offers less stretch than the original.

Elastic (rubber)

Natural rubber is made from latex, a milky substance (not the sap) secreted from various plants and trees. Natural rubber has been around since at least the time of the Mayan civilization. But it was not until the late 1870s, when the British established rubber plantations in Southeast Asia with seedlings stolen from Brazil, that the production of natural rubber became a major industry.

Among rubber's interesting properties are superb elongation (over 300 percent) and recovery. For producing shock (bungee) cord, sheets of rubber are sliced into thin ribbons that are then bundled to make the core.

ROPE CONSTRUCTION

Once the basic ingredients have been selected, it is up to the cook to assemble them—and a lot can be done in the kitchen to alter a recipe. Depending upon the rope, there might be just a few steps of twisting fibers and yarns, or there might be multiple steps of twisting, bundling, combining, weaving, coating, and heat treating.

Each stage of the process can be tweaked to slightly refine the final characteristics of the ropes. The designers must be careful to balance properties within the rope to prevent kinking, sheath slippage, and premature wear.

The distinction between cord and rope can be confusing since considerable overlap exists. The Cordage Institute, an international association of the rope industry since 1920, defines "cordage" as having a diameter of 1/16 inch to 3/8 inch (1.6 to 9.5 mm) and "rope" as having 3/16 inch to 5 inches (4.8 to 127 mm). What distinguishes one from another is the construction and, as a result, performance. Since this overlapping range of 5- to 9-mm diameter is common in the outdoor recreation world—and around the house—it is important to realize that differences may be considerable even if diameters are equal.

Although variations exist, most ropes can be classified as either "laid," in which strands of fibers are twisted together, or "braided," in which yarn bundles interweave. The kernmantle ropes so familiar to climbers are simply one type of braided construction; the term merely means "core/sheath."

Laid Ropes

For thousands of years, the basic method for making ropes remained virtually unchanged. Natural fibers were first spun counterclockwise (an S-twist) into yarns, then yarns were "formed" (twisted) clockwise (a Z-twist) into strands, and finally three strands (usually) were "laid" counterclockwise together to make a rope. Because the twists go in opposite directions at each step, the counteracting forces and friction hold the rope together and provide its strength.

Whenever you encounter a laid rope (photo 1.1), the odds are quite high that it will be built with this final counterclockwise twist.

Such a rope is commonly called "hawser-laid," but it is sometimes referred to as "right-handed." The opposite of a hawser-laid rope has a left-handed/clockwise twist. Called "shroud-laid," these usually have four strands instead of three, and are uncommon.

Before the age of machinery, ropes were built by hand . . . and foot. Since tall ships needed long, unspliced ropes, workers walked the yarns and strands between a fixed station and twisting hooks that were up to a thousand feet apart. According to one estimate, during a lifetime of rope making, a worker may have walked 25,000 miles—the circumference of the planet.

Laid ropes are usually fairly stiff and have a significant amount of stretch due to unwinding; different constructions and materials affect these properties. They can be easily spliced to connect ropes or make an eye, are inexpensive to produce, and are rugged; therefore, laid ropes remain popular for many heavy-duty and utility purposes. However, depending on material and stiffness, they often don't hold knots well. When handled improperly, laid ropes also have a tendency to "hockle" (a type of permanent damage from kinking that substantially weakens the rope; photo 1.2).

1.1 Laid Rope

Prior to the mid-1970s, laid ropes were still commonly used by climbers largely because they were about one-third less expensive than the fancy European kernmantle ropes. Plymouth Goldline was a "hard lay" rope designed in 1957 for mountaineering (it had a tighter twist than normal). These ropes could withstand a lot of abuse but stretched like crazy and made climbers spin dizzyingly when rappelling and prusiking in midair. Although every inch of Goldline can be easily

1.2 A hockle in a laid rope.

inspected for damage, its disadvantages have essentially relegated it to history; by definition, it cannot pass the climbing rope standards.

Braided Cord

"Braided cord" includes both the twine and small-diameter cordage of the kind you will typically find at the hardware store. The main differences between twine and cordage are longevity and strength. Twines, generally made from twisted or braided fibers such as cotton, jute, or polypro, are intended to be disposable, making them useful for tying parcels, gardening, baling hay, and so forth. The construction of cordage makes it generally more durable and stronger than twine. Smaller diameter cordage is typically made in one of three patterns—hollow braid, diamond braid, or solid braid—though these can also be used in larger ropes.

Hollow Braid: The hollow braid cords are the least-expensive cords and typically have eight, twelve, or sixteen strands that interweave. These lines can be easily spliced and are very flexible but tend to flatten when loaded. Although hollow braids are quite strong for their weight, they do not hold up well to abrasion since all the load-bearing fibers are exposed. (Photo1.3)

1.3 Hollow Braid, eight-strand

Diamond Braid: Using the same basic construction around a core of straight fibers produces a diamond braid, named for the appearance of the resulting sheath pattern. Diamond braid cords cannot be spliced and also flatten under load, but they are more abrasion resistant since the core carries some of the load. This construction allows different materials to be used in the core and sheath, so the desired qualities can be refined.

Solid Braid: A solid braid has nine, twelve, or eighteen strands that are tightly woven in an inter-

1.4 Solid Braid, 18-strand

locking pattern to form a very dense, round cord. Because they will not flatten under load, solid braids are well suited for use in pulleys (look at the sash cord on your window blinds for an example). These tend to be moderately strong and durable cords, though knots need to be set tight for good hold. (Photo 1.4)

Braided Ropes

Braided ropes offer the most strength and durability because many parts are optimized to work together. Although ropes have been braided by hand for ages, only in the mid-1800s was machinery invented to speed the process. Even with that technology, it was not until the 1950s, when nylon was readily available, that braided ropes began to grow in popularity. The 1970s was the boom era for braided rope technology as new materials and computer-controlled machinery became available.

Braiding a rope essentially creates a giant tube—what goes inside the tube, if anything, largely determines how the rope behaves. The options for cores include straight yarns, single braided strand, multiple braided strands, or multiple laid strands; some ropes even have a braided core within a braided sheath (photo 1.5).

Plaited: For larger diameter ropes, the simplest braided construction consists of four sets of double strands that interweave like in a maypole dance, with two going clockwise and two moving counterclockwise (other patterns are also possible). These are often called 8-strand plaited ropes; other names include square braid or square rope. They tend to be very flexible, resistant to kinking, and provide a good grip, making them popular for marine applications.

12-Strand Single Braid: Braiding a dozen individual strands (sixteen may be used in large ropes) makes the ropes round, so they handle better and are more durable, and may still be spliced.

Parallel Core: When all the fibers are straight, without any twists, the result is a rope with very little stretch. Often the core is encased in a plastic film before the sheath is braided. With limited ability to absorb shock, these ropes are one step away from wire cable, so

1.5 Braided Sheath, 48-bobbin

1.6 Kernmantle: cabled core within a braided sheath

their main application is for hoisting heavy loads when smooth running is needed (such as lifting stage sets in theaters and raising sails on sailboats).

Double Braid: One of the most significant advances in rope-building technology, a braid within a braid enables manufacturers to combine materials to achieve performances never before possible. Double-braided ropes received another boost in the 1980s when aramids and HMPE became available.

Double-braid construction is now used in a high percentage of ropes because it results in good handling, abrasion resistance, and UV protection for the core. Some of the early kernmantle climbing ropes were actually double braids, but they didn't absorb high-impact forces very well. Double braid is a common construction in accessory cords.

Stranded Core: Instead of one braided core strand, some ropes have three. This makes for a particularly durable rope that is still quite strong even if one of the core strands is cut by accident. Climbing ropes made with stranded core tend to have higher impact forces but greater longevity (Millet, formerly Rivory-Joanny, is one brand).

Cabled Core: The vast majority of dynamic climbing ropes use between six and twelve strands, with laid construction for the core. To balance the rope and resist kinking, half the "cables" are S-twist and the other half Z-twist. The physical unwinding of the twisted core strands gives this cabled core construction maximum stretch under high forces, which translates to the softest catch (lowest impact force) for falling climbers (photo 1.6). Most of these ropes now have a thin piece of colored plastic tape that identifies the year of manufacture.

CONSTRUCTION DETAILS

After the basics of choosing the materials and constructing the rope, each rope manufacturer can handle additional steps differently. These are the proprietary details that set one rope model apart from others of similar design.

Heat Set

When building a dynamic rope—that is, one that will absorb high impact forces—rope manufacturers select nylon 6 for its good elasticity. However, at some point during the manufacturing process, the nylon must be heated to about 250°F (120°C) to shrink it even further and maximize the elasticity.

Each manufacturer has its own heat-set method (temperature, time, dry versus steam), and these are closely guarded secrets. Some companies heat the yarns prior to construction, claiming this allows more control of the process; others heat the assembled rope, saying this balances the movement of core and sheath.

Low-elongation ropes, such as those used for climbing and caving, are not heat set because the flexibility of the molecules and the unwinding of twists is sufficient for moderate shock absorption.

Prestretching

For some rigging applications, any stretch is an undesirable rope characteristic. Yet low-stretch materials such as aramids are not always a good alternative because they are very expensive, may not have adequate flex fatigue, or the resulting line is too narrow to grip.

One solution is to prestretch the rope to remove as much natural give as possible. Usually this is done by tightly winding the rope on drums, which first tightens the braid and then removes the stretch of the material itself. Some companies instead "de-creep" ropes by slowly increasing the strain to about half the breaking load so that the fibers are not damaged. None of these prestretched or de-creeped ropes should be used for climbing or caving because they cannot handle surprise impacts.

Twist Rate

The amount of twist applied to the yarns and strands plays a major role in handling, durability, and shock absorption. Raw fibers from a giant spool are first twisted into S or Z yarns (photo 1.7); the size and number of the fibers determines the yarns' denier (weight). Next, another machine twists yarns into S or Z bundles (photo 1.8). The bundles are then either twisted into S or Z strands for the core or spooled onto bobbins for making the sheath (photo 1.9).

For core materials, more twist means more elasticity but too much means longer falls as the rope stretches. If the amount of clockwise and counterclockwise forces are not equal, the rope will handle terribly or

1.7 Twisting fibers into yarns

get weird bumpy sections inside. High modulus fibers (aramids, HMPE) must be carefully twisted with even tension and load sharing or the rope can essentially self-destruct inside; too much twist is also detrimental for these fibers.

For the sheath, the twist rate of the yarn bundles determines how the rope will feel and its durability. A high twist rate (more twists per inch) gives a firmer feel and helps prevent sheath slippage but results in the fibers reaching the surface more often. As these are cut from abrasion, the short sections fall out—the pile of fluff after a long rappel—and the rope retains its "new" look as the sheath gets thinner. A low twist rate means that the fibers are exposed less often, and when cut, they will stay in place. Thus ropes with less twist in the sheath get somewhat fuzzy with use, but the fibers stay in place to help protect the rest.

Sheath Construction

The coarseness and thickness of the sheath also affect durability, handling, and dynamic qualities. All of these factors are determined by the number of bobbins used to braid the sheath: the fewer the bobbins, the coarser and thicker the sheath and the less elastic the rope.

Typically, a 10.5-mm climbing rope is made with thirty-two, forty, or forty-eight bobbins (one company uses forty-four). If a rope has a

1.8 Twisting yarns into bundles

fine, tightly woven sheath, then it probably was braided with forty-eight bobbins and the sheath is 35 percent of the rope's weight. This rope will run smooth over the rock, resist dirt and water reaching the core, and provide a softer catch—but it won't last as long.

If the rope's sheath is very rough-looking, it is likely a thirty-two–bobbin design and the sheath accounts for about 40 percent of total rope weight. These ropes will withstand a great deal of abuse and are better for big walls, top roping, and gyms. Low-elongation ropes ("static" is a misnomer since they do stretch) used for caving and hauling on big walls generally have thirty-two–bobbin sheaths.

At the extreme end of the scale are arborist ropes, used daily for such abusive chores as lowering heavy branches. These tree ropes typically have a sixteen-bobbin sheath that is about half the rope's overall weight. The sheath is very thick, abrasion resistant, and provides a lot of friction, but the ropes also have less shock-absorbing ability.

Another factor of sheath design that affects rope performance is the tightness of the braid. Increasing the tension during braiding produces a firm sheath that is more abrasion and cut resistant, but also more prone to kinking. Decreasing the tension gives a supple rope that snakes nicely across rock and is easier to knot, but that has lower elongation. A few ropes, such as the Beal Program, have a sheath that is

1.9 Forty-eight bobbins dance around core strands to braid the sheath.

loose on the ends for ease of tying, firm for several meters where the ropes receive the most abuse from falls, and supple in the middle to reduce rope drag.

Some cheap ropes are made with a sheath that uses only Z-twist bundles. Although this saves a step during manufacture, it results in half the fibers running perpendicular to the direction of the rope. These will abrade much faster and create more drag than ropes with the sheath fibers oriented lengthwise with the rope.

Sheath Pattern

It is advisable to mark the middle of climbing ropes to speed setting up rappels and to help the belayer estimate how much rope is remaining. Unfortunately, tape will either fall off or slide out of place, and whipping creates a hard spot that doesn't feed well through a belay device. Many companies dye the middle of the rope, but this black area can be difficult to spot (especially on a dark rope) and tends to wear off after a while. Using marking pens runs a slight risk of damaging the nylon. (See Chapter 3 for more details.)

In the nicest climbing ropes, the pattern of the sheath changes at the halfway point—a very obvious and permanent method of marking the middle point. This is done by rearranging the bobbins on the braiding machine. However, it's an extra step, so bi-weave ropes cost more. A less satisfactory method (but still better than marking) involves splicing new colors into the sheath at the middle. The rope is plenty strong, but the splices are more prone to fuzzing and may create a thick spot in the sheath.

Some rescue ropes used by fire departments have reflective threads in the sheath for maximum visibility in the dark. This has trickled down to cordage and makes for great tent guylines that help prevent tripping in the dark. At least one model of caving rope is made with a glow-in-the-dark sheath that gives off light for ten hours.

Waterproofing Treatments

To paraphrase Benjamin Disraeli: there are lies, damn lies, and "waterproof" climbing ropes. A wet rope is heavier, weaker, abrades faster, cuts easier, and can freeze into an unmanageable cable. As mentioned earlier, the nylon 6 used in dynamic ropes absorbs more water than any other synthetic rope-making fiber; up to 9.5 percent by weight. This can be exacerbated by capillary action that draws more water in between the fibers. Because of this, rope manufacturers have developed various means of protecting ropes from water saturation—with varying degrees of success.

In the days when sailing ships used hemp ropes, the process of waterproofing was a nasty affair. Quality hemp was the strongest material, but salt water and sunlight degraded it. So the ropes had to be dipped in boiling tar before they were seaworthy.

The yarns of many dynamic climbing ropes are now coated with fluro chemicals such as polytetrafluoroethylene (PTFE-Teflon is one brand) prior to braiding. This treatment helps the fibers run smoothly through high-speed machinery during production and also improves the rope's performance. The slick coating allows the core fibers to slide smoothly against one another, reducing impact forces. As extra benefits, the nylon core becomes a bit more water resistant, the sheath is a tad more abrasion resistant, and the handling improves.

If coating all the individual fibers with PTFE were adequate to keep water out, companies would not need to offer "dry" ropes with an additional treatment that adds 10 percent to the cost. The second PTFE treatment (silicon and wax are no longer used for climbing ropes) to the sheath serves as a stopgap that reduces water entry and increases abrasion resistance. Companies who use treatments with a higher PTFE content produce costlier ropes that stay drier longer. But marketing hype and lack of a standardized test make it difficult to believe any of the claims.

Even the best treatments will wear off by the time the rope has fuzzed. This can be somewhat restored with a wash-in aqueous fluro chemical treatment (Nikwax or Sterling). But eventually, nylon ropes used for snow and ice climbing will get wet.

Recent tests by the Italian Alpine Club showed that wet ropes, even with a dry treatment, hold only one-third of the test falls as dry ropes; the thinner the rope, the worse the degradation. Due to technical limitations, there has never been a dynamic test of icy climbing ropes, but the indications suggest somewhat better dynamic performance (not handling) than wet ropes.

Rope Selection

When the mission is critical, always choose the best tool for the job. A basic understanding of materials and constructions used for ropes is important. But there are other considerations needed for proper selection—and to prevent potential calamities.

SELECTING UTILITY CORDAGE

For many camping, paddling, and household tasks, you need not spend extra for the nylon cordage commonly found in outdoor shops. While nylon may do the job, other, less expensive materials and constructions can be a better choice. (However, if there is any chance of severe shock-loading, nylon is the only material to consider.)

Start by deciding what material is most appropriate for the task. Polyester is popular for general purposes since it is strong and does not stretch too much. However, if price is a major consideration or the rope must float, polypro is a good candidate. Manila is fine for many utility purposes since it holds knots well. It also has a higher working temperature, making it a good choice if melting is a possibility. Sisal is weaker than other materials, but also cheaper, so it is practical for one-time use or when biodegradability is desirable.

The next issues to determine are the best diameter and, hand-in-hand, necessary strength for the task. Labels on packaged utility cord usually list both the size and the tensile strength. However, a strength rating is seldom provided for cordage on spools (look on the spool ends), so if you are purchasing cordage by the foot and strength is critical, you may need to consult the wholesaler's catalog (don't rely on a generic label as brands can vary significantly).

Often the construction method will be decided for you by the manufacturer and the store selection, though sometimes you'll have a choice. This is primarily a matter of how well the rope handles and how much it costs.

SELECTING SHOCK CORD

Because natural rubber degrades quickly in UV light, the sheath on better grades of shock cord are thickly braided polyester. This protects the core even when the cord is stretched. Nylon is another commonly used material for the sheath because of its elastic properties; however, it may not last as long outdoors as polyester. Polypro is found on the cheapest shock cord, but this stuff should stay indoors.

The thicker the cord's diameter, the greater the resistance to stretching. As a rule of thumb when you are using shock cord as a tie-down, you should not stretch the cord more than 75 percent beyond its normal length—and stretching it that much should require significant force. Rather than overstretching a shock cord, select a larger diameter or double it up.

SELECTING DYNAMIC CLIMBING ROPES

When Edelrid introduced the first kernmantle climbing ropes in 1951, an 11.0-mm rope could hold two falls (for a thorough discussion of rope testing, falling forces, and other esoterica, see my book *Rock & Ice Gear: Equipment for the Vertical World*, Mountaineers Books, 2000). The raw ingredient of dynamic ropes, nylon 6, hasn't changed in decades. Yet it is now common for 10.2-mm ropes to hold ten falls and there is even a 9.2-mm single rope that holds five falls. What's going on?

A lot of things as it turns out. None in themselves are major, but the cumulative effect is lighter, skinnier ropes that do more. Although the nylon molecule has not changed, the techniques for processing nylon into fibers have been improved, and finishes help even more. Computerized machines allow more sophisticated control over twisting, heat setting, and treatment. And many years of testing and experience have led to subtle refinements in manufacturing.

Using the Label

The hangtag on climbing ropes is one of the most widely read and least understood documents in an outdoor store. Few customers or salespeople truly know what the numbers mean or how to interpret them.

Before you start shopping, evaluate your needs. A light rope suitable for difficult sport climbs is a poor choice for a big wall climb or top roping. Twin ropes are great for ice climbs and alpine routes but a hassle for normal cragging.

Another factor in determining which rope to buy is the size of the climbers who will fall on it. Someone who is a hundred pounds dripping wet may be happier with a lightweight, smaller diameter rope, while a 200-pound climber is going to shred a skinny rope in no time and runs a much greater risk of cutting the line in a fall.

Unfortunately, lab tests don't tell the full story of how well a rope works in the field. Some ropes are designed to do little more than look good on tests. They are safe when used properly but may handle poorly and wear out quickly.

Type: Ropes intended for lead climbing fall into one of three categories: single (marked with a 1 inside a circle), half (marked with a 1/2 inside a circle), or twin (marked with two overlapping circles inside a circle). Both single ropes and a pair of twin ropes are used the same, clipped into each piece of protection as the climber moves upwards. A pair of half ropes are used by alternating which rope is clipped into the gear.

Single ropes are the most common and easiest to use. They are especially popular for rock climbing at developed crags and on big walls. Twin ropes come into their own on alpine climbs where the extra cut protection and sufficient length for long rappels are desirable.

There are many pros and cons for using half ropes, which require double rope technique, but they are at their best on wandering routes with dubious protection. Testing has shown double-rope technique reduces impact force on the top anchor by 30 to 40 percent compared to single-rope technique; this is mostly because of inefficiencies in belaying two ropes when only one is sliding.

Diameter and Mass: Most climbers use single ropes because they are the easiest to handle. Single ropes range in diameter from 9.2 to 11.0 mm, with 10.2 to 10.5 mm offering the best compromise of weight, handling, and durability. The sub–10-mm ropes are nice and light, but many have a relatively thin sheath, so they don't hold up well to lots of falls from heavy climbers; save these for difficult ascents where reduced weight and rope drag are more important than longevity.

Although it simplifies discussion, diameter is a poor method for selecting a rope because this number tells only one side of a complicated story. Referring to the mass (grams per meter) gives a better indication of what is in a rope. A 9.8-mm rope from one company could actually weigh more than the 10.0-mm rope from another.

Falls Held: Modern climbing ropes just don't break in the real world, so more test falls in a lab doesn't necessarily mean a safer rope. However, test fall rating does hint at a rope's durability, since the drops occur on the same section of rope. Standard ropes will survive between five and nine falls, while "multidrop" ropes hold ten to fifteen falls; the latter is a better choice for heavy-duty usage.

Impact Force: In theory, the impact force rating on a rope dictates how gentle the catch of a falling climber will be, so marketing departments and misinformed climbers place a lot of importance on this number. In reality, the belay device is the limiting factor on forces during a fall; in the vast majority of cases, it will slip before peak impact forces are achieved. The softer ropes make more of a difference when there is a lot of rope drag, typically when a climber is far from the belay, because friction increases the effective fall factor.

Sheath Percentage: Manufacturers increasingly are providing the sheath's percentage of the total weight. This is a useful indicator, though not conclusive, of durability and elasticity. A rope that is 45 percent sheath will hold up to abrasion better than one that is 33 percent.

Sheath Slippage: There used to be major problems with sheath and core of kernmantle ropes stretching at different rates. With better manufacturing processes, sheath slippage is seldom an issue anymore; simply trim the rope ends as necessary.

Sharp Edge Resistant: Recently, the *Union Internationale des Associations d'Alpinisme* (UIAA) created a new standard for a rope's resistance to cutting over a sharp edge. It is essentially the same as the fall test, but instead of a rounded orifice with a 10-mm radius (simulating a carabiner) in the drop test, the rope falls over a ninety-degree edge with a 0.75-mm radius. Though not a measure of durability (it is pass/fail and not an abrasion test), an edge-certified rope does indicate a burlier construction.

Static Elongation: Also called working elongation, this is how much the rope will stretch when a 176-pound (80 kg) person is rappelling, jumaring, or hanging while working a route; less is better.

Dynamic Elongation: The amount of stretch on the first fall used to be difficult to measure and was rarely reported. The maximum permitted stretch is 40 percent but most ropes are in the 30 to 35 percent range. This means if you are 15 feet above your last protection and fall, instead of 30 feet, you will travel about 40 feet before stopping! The higher dynamic elongation, the lower the impact force of the rope.

Rope Length

The standard length of climbing ropes has crept upward over the decades. In the early part of the last century, 100- to 120-foot ropes were common. In the 1960s and 1970s, most climbers used 150-foot (45-meter) ropes. In the '80s, 50-meter (165-foot) ropes became all the rage. And in the 1990s to present, 60-meter (200-foot) ropes have grown in popularity.

Does this mean you should get a 60- or even a 70-meter rope? Not necessarily. For single-pitch sport climbs, the extra length is often needed so that the climber can lower off from the top (this depends greatly upon the areas you climb). On long, multipitch climbs, a 60-meter rope allows an experienced team to combine older pitches and move more quickly. For alpine snow climbs, even a 100- or 120-meter half rope is not out of the question.

But long ropes are heavier, bulkier, and slower to coil. The greater distance between pitches means the leader must carry more gear; running out near the top is a common problem, often compounded by serious rope drag and poor communication with the belayer. And longer ropes are more prone to getting stuck on rappels. Believe it or not, it is usually as fast or faster for a team to use a 50-meter rope on most of the traditional multi-pitch climbs. Of course, it isn't as "manly" to use a short rope (or short skis, or short anything), so it is no surprise such ropes are fading in popularity.

SELECTING LOW-ELONGATION ROPES

If a rope will not be used for catching a falling lead climber, it is generally better to select one designed for reduced stretch. In order to absorb the energy of a fall, the dynamic rope necessarily trades off durability. Any elongation of the rope while hauling loads translates into more work. When ascending a hanging rope, the bounce of a dynamic rope creates a sawing action over rock edges. All bad things.

Although they are often called static ropes, in truth all of the ropes used in the outdoor world do stretch, so the term is misleading. According to the definition by the Cordage Institute, at 10 percent of its breaking strength, a "static" rope has less than 6 percent stretch while a "low-stretch" rope will give between 6 and 10 percent. But the UIAA standard specifies that a low-stretch rope must not elongate more than

5 percent with a 330-pound (150-kilogram) load. Another common term is "semi-static," but this too is vague.

Given the conflicting terminology, it is better to use the term "low elongation" when referring to the ropes you find in an outdoors shop. If you really need a static rope, go to a yachting supply store (with large bundles of cash in your pocket).

Types of Low-Elongation Ropes

Low-elongation ropes fall into three broad categories: nylon, nylon/polyester, and polyester. Knowing what the rope is made of gives the first hints as to how it will perform.

Nylon: Depending upon construction, the all-nylon, low-elongation ropes vary from some stretch (barely meets dynamic standards) to minimal stretch (falling is a *really* bad idea). Either nylon 6 or nylon 66 can be used, and heat treatment may or may not be applied to increase elasticity.

Most of the so-called "gym ropes" are nylon with a very beefy sheath (as much as 58 percent of the rope) that can withstand serious abuse. They typically stretch less than dynamic ropes but more than caving ropes. In a rock gym scenario, too much elongation means people hitting the floor and too little could result in anchor failure. Gym ropes address cost and liability concerns, but the average climber wouldn't want to take them outdoors.

Nylon low-elongation ropes are intended for caving and big wall climbing where some shock absorbency may be required in emergency situations, such as an anchor failure. These have much lower elongation than dynamic ropes, but many would survive at least one factor 1.7 test fall with a tolerable impact force.

These are also a good choice for top roping with the belayer on the ground because they are less expensive and more durable than dynamic ropes, plus the resting climber doesn't lose ground from rope stretch. It is also common to use 50 to 60 feet of low-elongation rope for rigging anchors at the top of cliffs; slip a couple lengths of 1-inch tubular webbing over the rope to improve sharp edge protection.

Nylon/Polyester: For greater durability, lower stretch, and somewhat better UV resistance, some ropes have a polyester sheath over a nylon core. This combination makes for a rugged rope that should handle sudden shock loads reasonably well. There is a greater potential for sheath slippage because of the two different materials, but otherwise these ropes handle about the same as others.

Polyester: When a minimum amount of stretch is required, such as for very long, free-hanging fixed lines, the rope will usually be made with a polyester sheath over a polyester core. In some cases, the core might be an aramid, HMPE, or liquid crystal polymer, but you will know by the exorbitant price. These ropes have the least shock absorbency and should be used only in situations where there is no chance of sudden impacts.

Comparing Low-Elongation Ropes

As Strother Martin said so well, "What we have heya is a failure to communicate." Unfortunately, low-elongation ropes fall under one testing standard in Europe and another in the United States. Because there are no labeling requirements in this country, the inconsistent data provided by manufacturers make it difficult to compare ropes.

In Europe, the low-elongation ropes cannot be sold unless they are certified and labeled as either Type A (most common) or Type B (reserved for special applications). In general, Type A ropes are between 10 and 10.5 mm; most are 10.5 mm. Type B ropes are between 8 and 9.9 mm, which makes them trickier to use with ascenders and descenders.

To achieve a Type A rating, the rope must survive five factor 1 falls with a 100-kilogram (220-pound) weight (very different from the dynamic rope test that is a factor 1.7 fall with an 80-kilogram (176-pound) weight). The impact force from a factor 0.3 fall and the same weight must be under 6 kilonewtons (kilonewton, or kN, is a measure of force: mass times acceleration). Again, this is very different from the dynamic standard that must not exceed 12 kN in a factor 1.7 fall. For Type B ropes, the mass is reduced to 80 kilograms. Furthermore, a Type A rope must hold at least 22 kN (4,945 pounds/force, or lbf) and a Type B must hold 18 kN (4,045 lbf); there is no load requirement for dynamic ropes. The labels provide additional information, such as what percentage of the rope's weight is in the sheath and how much the rope shrinks after a twenty-four hour soak in water.

Ropes that are ideal for caving, big wall climbing, and top roping are also well suited for use by rescue workers. In the United States, this means they fall under the domain of the National Fire Protection Association (NFPA), which sets its own standards for life safety ropes. Because this is a *huge* market—think about how many ropes every rescue squad, fire department, and SWAT team around the country go through each year—the big gorilla makes the rules.

Therefore U.S.–made low-elongation ropes are built in fraction-of-an-inch diameters (not metric) and mass is stated as pounds per 100-foot section (rather than grams/meter). You will typically see tensile strength but not impact force or number of falls held. The working load limit (WLL) or safe working load (SWL)—same thing—is merely the strength divided by a safety factor of fifteen.

Dynamic Versus Low-Elongation

Two decades ago, climbing ropes were pretty straightforward: They were dynamic or not. And that dichotomy permeated the literature and many people's thinking. These days, however, ropes are much more fine-tuned to specific applications.

Without question, if the rope will be used for lead climbing, it must be dynamic to avoid serious injury. However, tests by the UIAA showed that top roping and rappelling rapidly diminish a dyanamic rope's shock-absorbing capabilities. Save your good dynamic ropes for lead climbs and use either a low-elongation rope or a retired dynamic rope for top-roping climbs. The latter may be the cheapest option, but an old lead rope will cause the resting climber to lose some ground due to stretch.

For ascending vertical fixed lines in a cave or on a big wall, as well as for hauling heavy loads, the less stretch the better; both for efficiency and safety. Using a dynamic rope would mean a lot more work just to get off the ground, as your body weight pulls several extra feet of rope down. Even worse, your movements while ascending saw the rope back and forth over rock edges. The standard 10- to 10.5-mm low-elongation ropes (Type A) are the best choice and still have enough give that you stand a chance of survival in case of unexpected shock loading.

Use only the specialty low-elongation (Type B) and true static ropes for demanding applications such as extreme caving and high altitude climbing, where the risks are fully understood and appreciated. While lighter and more compact, their reduced cut resistance and ability to absorb shock are major concerns.

Mixed Ropes

On the other hand, a skinny low-elongation line can be an ideal accompaniment to a single dynamic rope on long, multipitch climbs. This system allows the leader to climb with the single rope and use the skinny rope as a "tag line" with an end clipped to the back of the harness. Once the leader reaches the belay, or even mid-pitch in some cases, the tag line can haul up a pack or gear.

When it is time to go down, the tag line becomes the second rappel rope for full-length raps. Because one rope may be a 10.2-mm and the other an 8.0-mm, they will stretch at different rates, so it is a good idea to make the tag line extra long (65 meters if the single is 60). Although a 7-mm rope is more compact, its lightness allows it to blow around too much in the wind, so the skinnier line is not recommended.

When rigging the rappel, put the tag line through the anchor and place the knot on the single rope side. This prevents the knot from getting pulled into the anchor as the skinny rope stretches, which could mean a stuck rope. It also means you have more of the good rope in hand, in case your ropes get stuck anyway and you must lead up to fix the problem.

SELECTING ACCESSORY CORD

When it comes to purchasing accessory cord, it is mostly a matter of guesswork, since few manufacturers provide much information. Ropes between 4 and 8 mm can be UIAA certified, but this only measures tensile strength and mass. No testing is required for elasticity, shock absorption, or anything else.

In most cases, accessory cord probably has a nylon sheath with a nylon laid core construction, since that is what climbing rope companies are geared up to make. However, they can use polyester instead, or a braided core, since these cords have less elongation.

For slinging chocks and making cordelettes, many climbers prefer the low bulk of accessory cord with an aramid or HMPE core. This requires a diameter of only 5 or 5.5 mm to achieve the strength of 8-mm rope with a nylon core. A smooth sheath with a tight braid offers good handling and makes it easy to cinch knots snug.

When selecting cord for Prusik slings, choose a diameter 3 to 4 mm smaller than the rope it will grab. For a 10- to 11-mm rope, a 6- or 7-mm sling works well, but narrower diameter is difficult to release and cord that is too stiff will not grab well. Some companies now offer cord designed for this application that has a rougher sheath for grip and a nylon cable core to absorb shock (potentially an issue in rescues).

Canyoneers visiting remote canyons sometimes use rappel anchors made of 10- to 12-mm manila rope. This should be strong enough for one-time use (test first!) and will eventually rot away. If you encounter such an anchor, do not trust it!

> ### CAUTION
>
> Never lower a person with the rope running over webbing or cord ... it *will* melt through from the intense friction. This happens fastest on webbing with HMPE, but it doesn't take much longer with all-nylon webbing and cord. Tests have shown that lowering a 176-pound (80-kilogram) climber will melt through brand-new 8-mm nylon accessory cord in less than 13 feet (4 meters). Bottom line: Always use a running rope over metal.

SELECTING WEBBING

Webbing is a good alternative to rope when thinner material is required or loads need to be distributed over a wide area. Climbers prefer webbing for making runners because of its low bulk and high strength. Webbing is also great for strapping boats on top of a car or lashing gear in a raft because strong aluminum buckles greatly simplify the task.

Although webbing has many uses, it is important to realize that webbing is nowhere near as abrasion resistant as rope. One study showed that 1-inch nylon webbing had only a quarter the abrasion resistance of 9-mm dynamic rope with the same tensile strength.

Webbing Materials

Just about any material that can be made into rope can also be made into webbing. A variety of fibers is used for nonclimbing webbing; for example, polypro is common for tie-down webbing and polyester is now used for nearly all seatbelts.

Nylon has long been the material of choice for use in climbing webbing because of its strength and elasticity. Any webbing purchased off the spool at an outdoor shop should be nylon (ask to be sure, especially if it is very cheap).

To decrease bulk and weight, HMPE is often blended in sewn climbing webbing. This material, easily identified by the white color since it does not take dye, allows much smaller webbing to hold the same force as traditional nylon webbing. The HMPE is too slick to hold a knot, however, so it is not sold in bulk to consumers. The slickness and low melting point of HMPE also make these runners a poor choice for use in friction knots.

Webbing Construction

Rope is produced by twisting and braiding fibers together so that friction holds them together. Webbing, on the other hand, is made by weaving fibers on a loom, much like fabric; indeed, webbing is called "narrow fabric" by the industry that makes it.

For webbing, the strength comes from fibers that run the entire length of the material (called the warp). Fibers that run across the width of the webbing (called the weft or fill) hold it together. Altering the weave results in various patterns, but this is more of a cosmetic than a performance issue.

Solid versus Tubular

Webbing can be woven either as a solid narrow fabric or as a hollow tube that lies flat. (All webbing is flat, so this term has little meaning and should be avoided in discussing webbing.) Sometimes it is difficult to distinguish solid from tubular webbing just from appearance.

Solid webbing can be very thin (usually called tape), fairly thin (such as on seatbelts and straps on a pack), or quite thick (as on the webbing used to hoist boats). For a given width of webbing made from the same material, strength is directly correlated with thickness. But thick or thin, solid webbing tends to be rather stiff and it often does not hold knots particularly well—they need to be checked often.

Tubular webbing (photo 2.1) is more supple than solid webbing and holds knots better. Because it consists essentially of two sheets of fabric, it distributes forces well when it is loaded over an edge. With solid webbing, more stress builds on the outer surface than the inner, so the webbing is more prone to cutting over a sharp corner. These characteristics make tubular webbing the choice of climbers for use as runner material.

Rescue teams favor thick 1-inch solid webbing because it is stronger than the standard 1-inch tubular webbing (6,000 pounds versus 4,000 pounds). It is also more abrasion resistant and is less affected by small cuts, yet it costs the same. All of this is great in the rescue world, but the solid webbing is overkill for climbing: It is too stiff, too bulky, and it unties too easily.

Chain versus Spiral Weave

Up until the 1980s, most tubular webbing in the United States was produced by spiral weaving on shuttle looms. The resulting webbing was strong, but the looms were slow. Also, such spiral weave webbing

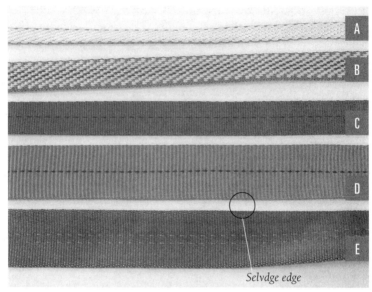

2.1 Tubular Webbing: A) 8-mm HMPE/nylon, B) 15-mm nylon/HMPE/polyester, C) ¹¹⁄₁₆" climbing spec nylon, D) 1" mil-spec nylon, E) 1" climbing spec nylon

can unravel like a sweater if the ends are not carefully melted. It does not have any seams that can abrade and, for a time, it was required to meet military specifications (mil-spec).

Most shuttle looms have now been replaced by more sophisticated needle looms (also called shuttleless looms) that make a chain weave and are four times faster. Webbing from France, the other leading supplier, has long been made on needle looms.

The early versions of chain weave webbing had a knit seam that ran along one edge which, if cut, could severely weaken the webbing. However, chain weave webbing has come a long way in the past decades—so much so that the 1-inch mil-spec webbing is now considered the cheap stuff—adequate but inferior to most other climbing webbing. The newer chain weaves feature a lock stitch along one edge (called a selvedge edge) that will not unravel if damaged.

In Europe, regulations require that nylon webbing have a colored stripe on one side for each 5 kN (1,124 lbf) that it will hold in a tensile test. Thus webbing that is rated to 18 kN (4,045 lbf) has three stripes. (This rule does not apply to webbing made with HMPE because it cannot take a dye and is sold only on sewn products that have labels attached.) There is no such regulation in the United States, so webbing often has a single stripe of black or yellow in the center to appease the military (it has no significance).

> ### CAUTION
>
> According to both military and commercial standards, webbing that is sold on a spool can have up to three splices. The only thing holding the ends together is a piece of masking tape! At least one climber has died from failure to inspect the webbing—don't become another statistic.

Making Runners

A runner is a loop of webbing, or cord, made by tying the ends together. Also called slings, these loops are great for extending gear placements so the climbing rope will run smoothly with less friction. Runners are also handy for building anchors to set up a top rope, improvising a sit or chest harness, and a multitude of other tasks.

The webbing sold on spools for climbing is made of nylon. For decades, the standard runner material was 1-inch (25-mm) tubular webbing; this is still favored by schools and rescue teams because it is cheap and plenty strong (17 to 20 kN). Most climbers now prefer the thick 11/16-inch (18-mm) tubular webbing, often called super tape; it is plenty strong (13 to 16 kN) and costs the same but is more compact. Narrower tubular webbing such as 9/16-inch (14-mm) only holds about 10 kN, while 1/2-inch (13-mm) holds only half that; save these for special applications, not everyday use.

In theory, a loop would be as strong as two pieces of webbing. Although proper stitching is supposed to equal the strength of the webbing itself, there is enough variance to cause a slight loss in strength. Unlike a straight piece of webbing that is pulled between giant drums, loops are tested between two pins the diameter of a carabiner (10 mm); these also reduce strength. In actuality, sewn webbing runners test about 10 percent weaker than twice the webbing's tensile strength.

Using water knots produces a wide range of results because of considerable variability of stresses. On average, knotted runners test about 73 percent of the strength of sewn runners. However, due to the high degree of stress variance, knotted runners would be rated at just 57 percent of the sewn runners if the same statistical system (3 sigma) used for climbing equipment was applied. Thus sewn runners offer greater strength with less bulk, while knotted runners are less expensive and can be untied.

Rope Care

Considering that dynamic single ropes cost between $.75 and $1.45 per foot, it is understandable why climbers want them to last as long as possible. Low-elongation ropes used for caving are less expensive (about $.53 to $.68 per foot) but subject to a much nastier environment. Some basic TLC will ensure you get the most value, and safety, from your ropes.

Although much of this chapter is intended for climbers, the basic principles of preserving ropes apply to other pursuits. The sections on Cutting Ropes, Rope Protection, Removing Kinks, and Storage apply to all rope users.

NEW ROPES

Obtaining the best performance from a climbing rope starts as soon as you get it home. Excited new rope owners often improperly uncoil the rope, throw away the hangtag, and rush to climb without proper preparation . . . then get frustrated when it handles poorly.

Uncoiling

When a rope comes off of the braiding machine, it is "neutral"; that is, there are no inherent kinks or twists in the sheath or core. Next, the manufacturers make hanks of rope, essentially by winding the rope up on a wheel. After this step, the rope is still neutral. Finally, the new owner unwraps the finishing knot and then, loop by loop, flakes the rope onto the ground. The rope is now horribly kinked and the new owner is irritated at the company.

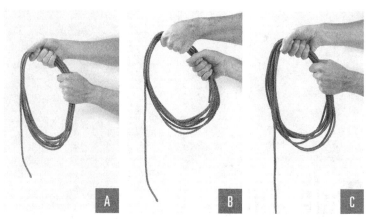

3.1 Uncoiling a new rope, hand-over-hand

The way to avoid this mess is to unroll the rope by rotating the coil until the entire length is lying on the ground; this keeps the rope twist free and neutral (photos 3.1.A, B, C). This simple, one-time procedure costs a few extra minutes but saves a lot of headaches. Once the rope is all stacked, find the ends and butterfly coil the rope (see Butterfly Coil, Chapter 4).

Preliminary Steps

It is a good idea to file away the hangtag—after you read it—so that you have a record of when the rope was purchased, the model, and the serial number. This information will be important if you must contact the manufacturer about a problem.

If you manage a number of ropes for a club, school, or rescue team, then it is best to use about 2 inches of clear heat-shrink tubing to secure a label to one end. Use waterproof ink and list the diameter, type (dynamic or static, standard or dry), length, and date. Avoid using codes, since anyone should be able to understand this curriculum vitae.

For best performance and longevity, new caving ropes should be preshrunk prior to use. Soak the rope in clean water until bubbles stop rising, drain, then pull through a rappel device that is anchored. Repeating this pulling process two or three times (pulling from the same end) helps stabilize the rope by tightening the sheath and core together. Some sheath slippage may be expected, but once the rope is trimmed off, it should remain stable. Thoroughly dry the rope by hanging it in a shady spot before storing.

Measuring

Ropes shrink—sometimes a lot. When a climbing rope is cut at the factory, it is generally about 2 percent longer than marked on the tag. This is to ensure that it is the proper length by the time it reaches the consumer. When conducting reviews of ropes, I have measured many that were a couple feet longer than advertised but also a few that were shorter than promised (one was 48 meters instead of 50).

It is worth finding out exactly what you have. Don't trust the label—the difference could be fatal when rappelling and lowering on sport climbs. For convenience, you can double the rope and then double it again before measuring and multiplying by four (not exact but reasonable).

However, all ropes continue to shrink with use: Dirt, falls, weathering all add up. On average, a climbing rope will shrink about 5 to 10 percent depending upon usage in the field. So that rope we thought was 50 meters but was actually 48 meters could possibly end up less than 45 meters long—that's 16 feet shorter than expected! Bottom line: It is worth checking the rope length at least once a year . . . the life you save may be your own.

Cutting Ropes

Cutting a rope is no great mystery—any sharp knife will do. However, there are some tricks to ensure a neat job, and some core materials require their own procedures. To start with, firmly wrap the section to be cut with a piece of tape (electrical, athletic, even masking tape will work). Cut through the center of the tape, leaving the remaining tape in place. This holds the rope fibers together and results in a clean cut.

Most outdoor shops and many hardware stores have a hot cutter that is fast and efficient; if you take your own rope in, they will gladly let you use the cutter or do it for you. Or you can buy a soldering iron with a cutting blade for about $20. Some people heat up an old knife on a stove, which does just as good a job. But none of these methods are necessary. Just tape the rope and use a really sharp knife (straight, not serrated edge) on a cutting board. Even aramid will slice with little trouble. Avoid scissors since they tend to mangle the cut.

After you have cut a rope down to size, seal the fresh ends to prevent unraveling. That's where a hot cutter or hot knife is convenient: You can use it to seal a standard rope in one easy step. (These won't work on aramid since it doesn't melt.)

For synthetic ropes, melt the fibers together with a lighter. Do this in a well-ventilated area. Get a good glob of molten material, but remove the flame if the rope catches fire. Mush the glob together on a cool surface, such as a metal plate (using your fingers on hot melted plastic yields predictable results: burned digits). Often you need to reheat the ends once or twice to ensure that all the fibers are bonded.

Since aramid will not melt, you need a different technique for sealing ropes with that core material. After cutting the rope, slide the sheath back and trim off a half inch of the aramid core. Then milk the sheath back into place so that it extends beyond the core. Melt the sheath down until it forms a solid blob on the ends of the core. Tamp the hot material right into the aramid fibers.

Sometimes it can be difficult to force cord through the holes in climbing stoppers and hexes. In that case, use the above trick but cut back even more core and seal the sheath end so it makes a point with a section that has no core. Pull the cord through the holes (needle-nose pliers help) and then trim the point and seal the end properly.

Climbing ropes always have the ends sealed and a piece of tape wrapped around the ends to mark the type and length. Inexplicably, some companies use black tape or a color that matches the rope. Dumb: We *want* to find the ends in a pile easily! Replace their tape with something bright (fluorescent even) but do not make it too long or bulky since it could catch in an anchor as a rappel is pulled.

Marking Ropes

A topic of endless debate among climbers is how to mark the middle of a rope. Some people don't bother, out of fear of possible damage from chemicals, while others mark the quarter and halfway points so the belayer can estimate how much rope remains.

The safest solution is to purchase bi-pattern ropes (see Sheath Design, Chapter 1), though they cost a few dollars more. Some companies mark the rope's center at the factory with tape or black dye. The major problem with tape is that it doesn't last and, instead of falling off, it can slide out of position. Do yourself a favor and remove tape. Whipping is a poor choice because the rigid spot produced on the rope makes belaying and rappelling more difficult.

The core of the debate is whether chemicals in marking pens (Marks-A-Lot, Sharpie, laundry pens) can damage the nylon of the rope. A study by the German Alpine Club set out to prove this is the case. They managed to find some deterioration, but the testing situation was so extreme that the results should not cause alarm. However, based on this study, the UIAA Safety Commission has recommended against marking ropes with pens unless it comes from the same company that makes the rope.

If you want to be sure your ropes aren't weakened in the slightest, do not mark them at all. Those who prefer the convenience and greater safety of having the marks can take solace in knowing that there are no reported cases of a rope breaking (or the sheath even wearing faster at a marked spot) in North America. Personally, I will continue to mark my ropes with pens sold by the rope companies.

EDGE PROTECTION

Even if you are not a climber, protecting ropes from sharp edges and rough rock just makes sense. Due diligence ahead of time can save a lot of expense and, possibly, grief.

When setting up top ropes, pay careful attention to how the anchor lines run. Try to locate the anchor point (always two locking carabiners) so that the climbing rope will not rub against the rock. In some cases, a bad anchor set-up can trash a rope in a single afternoon of climbing.

When fixing lines in caves or on big walls, or rigging top rope anchors, it is smart to position a rope guard wherever there are sharp edges. This is typically a 1- to 2-foot-long tube of rugged material, such as canvas, that fastens around the rope with Velcro and is held in place by a string tied to the rope; a coiled urethane sleeve is more convenient (photo 3.2).

The rope guard can be a nuisance to pass while ascending or descending, but it's better than a cut rope sending you to oblivion. Climbers sometimes use duct tape over sharp edges, but this probably doesn't offer much protection. The best solution for fixed lines is to install intermediate anchors (called re-directs) so that sections of rope are loaded for less time.

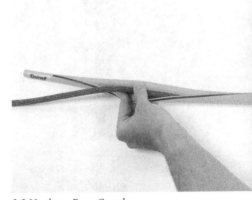

3.2 Urethane Rope Guard

For spelunking into caves with drops deep inside, pack the ropes in rope bags to keep them clean until needed; they will last longer without mud ground in. If it's a wet cave, put the ropes inside trash bags to keep them dry.

In alpine environments, it is common to pull down a few rocks along with your rappel rope. Do yourself a favor and shelter as much of the rope as possible before giving that last tug. It's a real drag to have a ten-pounder land on your expensive rope . . . especially when you have a few more rappels to go!

Use a slow, steady pull on the rappel line until the moment the end clears the anchor. Then give a quick outward tug so the rope falls away from the rock. If you tug fast too soon, the end of the rope might self-tie into a half hitch at the anchor, and you'll have a stuck rope.

PREVENTING KINKS

Kinks are the bane of all climbers and anyone else who works with ropes. As discussed above (see Uncoiling, earlier in this chapter), many climbers unknowingly put dozens of kinks into their brand-new ropes when they unwrap them the first time. However, even if you get this step right, many of the things you do in everyday practice can induce the evil kinks to emerge and taunt you.

3.3 *Figure-Eight Rappel*

Many climbers blame the figure-eight rappel device for twisting rope into an unmanageable beast. In fact, this is another case of improper usage. Holding the brake hand off to the side is the culprit; in effect the device becomes a worm gear for twisting ropes. Instead, keep the brake hand below the figure eight so that the rope above and below are parallel and everything remains copacetic (photo 3.3).

Similarly, the Munter hitch is often accused of severely kinking ropes, particularly if used for a rappel, but this is another case of pilot error. It will add twists only when the brake hand is held off to the side—really! Prove this to yourself by gripping the rope tightly as it runs under tension through a Munter and you will feel the twists building up only when the rope is not parallel.

When a rope is brand new, the core and sheath are both twist free (neutral). As the sheath is braided around the core, a pattern is formed that is not noticeable in normal handling. However, when running under high pressure across a surface, this sheath pattern can act like rifling in a gun's barrel and cause rotation of the rope. Particularly with ropes that have a rugged sheath (32 bobbin braid), this is where some of those unexplained kinks come from after a long lower or rappel.

The first couple of times that you rappel on a rope, it may want to twist in your hand. Instead of allowing the twists to pass through the rappel device, clamp the rope tight and walk your hands down the rope as you descend so that twists are forced out the end. After a few uses, the core and sheath achieve a set and the rope tends to stay neutral.

Avoid using carabiners with a flattened cross-section for belaying, rappelling, and top-rope anchors. These tend to make ropes twist more than carabiners with a large, rounded rope-bearing surface. And if using a Munter hitch, be sure to select a pear-shaped locking carabiner instead of a D to prevent pinching.

Rappel anchors can be another culprit. If two bolts are horizontal to each other and the rope is run through both, kinks will result; instead, the bolts should be connected by a chain or sling with a rappel ring in the center. When retrieving the rope after a rappel, be certain to pull on the side that is closer to the rock or mayhem may result (stuck rope from kinks or the taped end getting pinched between rock and anchor). If two ropes are joined, the knot goes on the side of the rappel ring nearer the rock.

When hauling loads on a wall, you can save a lot of grief by using a quality swivel (such as the Petzl) atop the haul bag. This spinning connector allows the bag to rotate as it pendulums across the rock without twisting the rope.

The method used for coiling ropes is also a major factor in kink formation. (For coiling methods, see Chapter 4.)

REMOVING KINKS

Okay, so the nasty gremlins have gotten into your rope. How do you exorcise them? There are many rituals that work, but it is basically a matter of pulling the rope through a friction device or your hands numerous times so that the twists go out the unattached end.(Muttering incantations and shouting "Demons be gone!" is optional.) Given a cliff of sufficient height, a free-hanging single-rope rappel will do the trick (if the above mistakes are not made). Or you can anchor a tube-style belay device and pull the rope all the way through two or three times until it no longer twists.

Another method for on-the-fly kink removal is to whip the rope up and down so that you create a series of big sinusoidal waves. This allows the kinks to propagate toward, and right out, the end.

PULLEYS

If a rope will routinely be used with a pulley, the inner diameter of the sheave (the pulley wheel) should be at least five rope diameters (for 10-mm rope, use a 5-cm pulley). For nylon and polyester rope, an 8:1 ratio is preferable, both for hoisting efficiency (bigger is easier) and rope longevity. However, ropes with an aramid core require a 20:1 ratio to prevent internal damage.

Climbers are generally reluctant to carry large rescue pulleys so they compromise with a smaller size. Do yourself a favor and select a model with sealed ball bearings instead of a bronze bushing; it hoists easier and lasts longer. Models with built-in ratchets are ideal for hauling loads on walls and for crevasse rescue. (Photo 3.4)

WASHING

Occasionally, climbing ropes become so soiled that they need to be cleaned; caving ropes routinely need a good wash. I've tried a variety of methods and now prefer machine washing. Some argue that T-shaped rope washers that attach to a garden hose can drive dirt particles deeper into the rope, but the effect is likely minimal.

Before washing, chain-stitch the rope (see Chain Stitch, Chapter 4, Rope Management) to prevent tangles. Next, place it in a mesh stuff sack to keep the rope from wrapping around the agitator of a top-loader (not necessary if the machine is a front-loader).

Use cold water to minimize shrinkage; warm water may be used if the rope is very dirty. Mild soap (NikWax Tech Wash or Woolite) is preferred. However, if the rope is heavily soiled, a detergent that does not contain bleach or bleach substitutes (Ivory Snow) can safely lift away the grime. A small amount of fabric softener can improve the handling of older ropes, and reduce impact forces, by restoring lubricants that have worn away. If the rope's water repellency has diminished, or was never there, you can use a wash-in treatment (NikWax Rope Proof or Sterling ProArid) to improve wet performance.

Do not use a clothes dryer unless you are applying a water repellent treatment (required to make it bond, follow directions carefully). Simply air dry the rope in a shaded spot by loosely hanging loops over a clothesline or furniture.

STORAGE

Though synthetic fibers are resistant to rot and mildew, it is prudent to dry them before storage. Stow ropes in a nice cool place where they are protected from sunlight and moisture. As discussed in the first chapter, various chemicals can degrade some rope materials. Certainly do your damnedest to guard lifelines from contamination—better safe than sorry.

The major concern is that acids can attack and degrade nylon with no visible damage. Within the past twenty years, nine climbing ropes are known to have failed because of acid contamination, several with fatal results. Be especially vigilant about car batteries (sulfuric acid)

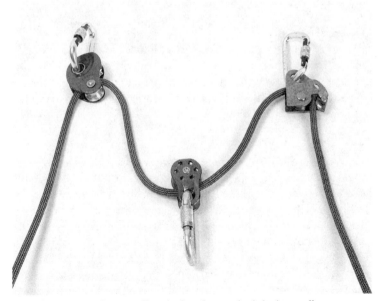

3.4 Pulleys: two ratcheting pulleys (top) and a standard climbing pulley

and muriatic acid (used for cleaning bricks). Even the fumes can be injurious. An acid-exposed rope can break with very little force and leaves a telltale sign only after the fact.

Some cars' batteries are located in the trunk but this should not be a problem. Though you shouldn't make a habit of storing climbing ropes in any car trunk (they can get mighty hot), there is no danger from sulfuric acid vapors causing harm, assuming a properly maintained, sealed battery (nonsealed batteries are less common these days).

Other big no-no's include: household bleach, peroxide bleach, pool chlorine, and drain cleaners. If even a hint of contamination is possible from any of these at full strength, chop the rope up into unusable pieces.

Fortunately, the list of things you don't have to worry about is a lot longer. It includes insect repellent (DEET), sunscreens, white gas, vegetable oil, vinegar, fruit juice, and blood and other body fluids (aside from contagion risk). Rinse these off and the rope will be fine.

If the ropes have been exposed to seawater, rinse them thoroughly to remove the salt. Otherwise the sharp crystals can lead to internal damage and increase impact forces. Simply air dry the rope and webbing in a shaded location after the rinse.

LONGEVITY

The age-old question among climbers and cavers is "How long does a rope last?" Short answer: Nobody knows, but err on the side of caution. For some reason, that standard reply isn't good enough when it comes to spending $100 to $200 on a new rope and the old one looks just fine.

Age

The question about safety is particularly relevant to someone who purchased a climbing rope and used it a couple of times, or perhaps never even took it out of the bag. Then a baby comes along, a major health problem intervenes, or a job gets in the way, and the rope goes into the closet for several years or even decades. When the owner is ready for more joy, that old rope is tempting—but is it still trustworthy?

When this concerns unused ropes, the discussion breaks down into two questions: How much strength does a rope lose over time? And how much elasticity does a rope lose over time?

It is fairly obvious that a rope doesn't get any stronger after it has been produced. The data from tensile tests of old ropes is somewhat conflicting, but the general consensus is that strength loss is minimal (2 percent per year) to nonexistent. Nearly everyone agrees that a properly stored, unused rope, even if twenty years old, will not break if used as designed.

Where the issue gets sticky is the dynamic capacity of old climbing ropes. The concern is that greater impact forces will be imparted to both climbers and their protection. Also, if elasticity decreases, so does resistance to cutting over an edge. Several studies have shown a decrease in the number of falls held by older, unused ropes. This is the reason companies recommend against using ropes over five years old for lead climbing—not to sell more ropes.

Pitt Schubert, who has worked more than thirty years for the German Alpine Club and who is chairman of the UIAA Safety Commission, investigated many old ropes. According to him, "Some of these ropes were fifteen, twenty, twenty-five, and even thirty years old. They were tested by a UIAA-approved test laboratory. The result: All ropes held one fall; and no rope broke in the knot.

The bottom line is that if they have been properly stored, old but new-looking ropes are *probably* fine for top roping and rappelling. However, for lead climbs where forces can be much higher, it is smart to rely on fresher ropes. If in doubt, cut it up or throw it out.

Mileage

Age may not be a major factor in determining rope life, but usage is an entirely different matter. Extensive data show that repeated short falls, whether sport climbing or top roping, quickly wear out dynamic ropes—owners of climbing gyms know this all too well. Likewise, frequent rappelling, particularly on dirty ropes, does a lot of damage. One study showed that just fifty rappels with a figure-eight device reduced the number of falls held by a third.

In theory, climbers and cavers should keep a log of usage for each of their ropes—yeah, right. Perhaps a few manage this task, but the vast majority of climbers never bother. (On the other hand, keeping a rope log is mandatory for schools and rescue teams since no single person knows the history.)

It is impossible to predict how long a rope will last because of all the variables. For example, your local crags make a big difference: coarse granite abrades ropes much faster than smooth limestone.

Heavy climbers do more wear and tear than light climbers. Frequent falls and lowering wallop a rope more than occasional falls when traditional climbing.

Tests of ropes with known histories indicate that after one hundred 50-meter pitches, a climbing rope loses half of its fall rating. And another 120 pitches (11,000 meters of climbing total) reduces dynamic ability to one third of original. So a well-used nine-fall rope might survive only three drops on a test machine.

At first glance, that reduction in a rope's dynamic ability may seem alarming. But consider this: According to Pit Schubert, "Because the fall on the UIAA-test-machine is much stronger than in the real world (in practice no rigid falling mass, no static belay), it is not possible for a rope which holds one fall on the UIAA-test-machine to break in practice—not in the knot, not in the running belay, not at the belaying device, only when the rope is loaded over a sharp edge. And this happens very, very seldom."

Schubert's data shows that in Germany and Austria, between 1969 and 1982, twelve ropes failed, all by cutting over a sharp edge. Yet in the past twenty years (1983 to 2003), only two ropes failed over an edge. He attributed part of the reason to better single rope designs and part to greater use of twin ropes for alpine climbing.

Evaluation

Ultimately, the decision on when to retire a rope comes down to an educated guess and gut instinct unless you've kept a rope log. Experienced climbers constantly inspect their rope as they belay, both looking and feeling for signs of damage.

It is important to understand that even a fifteen-fall rope can be damaged by a single hard fall in the real world. If a rope is subjected to a fall factor greater than 1, it must be carefully inspected by applying some tension and feeling the entire length. Any weird lumps, bumps, or depressions in the core are grounds for immediate retirement; core strands can be kinked or broken. A stiff section in the core indicates that nylon fibers have melted together from absorbing energy of a fall.

The best indicator of rope condition is a careful inspection of the sheath fibers. A definite connection exists between the number of cut fibers and the reduction in rope performance. If half of the sheath yarns are abraded, it is time to get a new rope.

If a rope is used for sport climbing, the sheath will experience major wear about 6 feet (2 meters) from each end. This is due to frequent short falls while the climber is working out routes. Some climbers extend the life of their rope by purchasing an extra-long model and cutting off the ends once the sheath starts thinning. However, the resulting rope is not the same as a fresh rope, and impact forces will be greater.

Although climbers have been admonished never to step on a rope, it actually does no significant damage. Not that I recommend the practice or would let you stand on *my* ropes. And a rope that has been hit by rockfall must have every inch carefully inspected.

Even stabbing a crampon or ice axe through the rope does not severely weaken it as long as the point is parallel with core fibers. Though a speared rope should be retired when you get home, it should be safe to finish up the ascent or descent if most of the core and sheath are intact.

WEBBING CARE

Since webbing is made from the same materials as ropes, the basics of rope care fully apply. There is less concern about degradation with age because shock absorbency is not a major function; nylon runners have some give, but minor compared to the rope, and HMPE runners are static. Properly stored runners should retain their strength for a

---

CAUTION

When retreating from alpine climbs, it is common to rappel off of webbing tied around a rock or tree. This is perfectly safe if the webbing is new because the rope is not running. However, when the rope is pulled down afterwards, the friction can do serious damage to the webbing (especially if there was a lot of rope drag). When you encounter old rappel anchors that do not have rappel rings, there is a good chance the webbing has been severely weakened. Inspect the webbing very carefully on the inner surface and replace or back it up if you have even a hint of doubt.

If it is likely others will follow your descent line, install two aluminum (or one stainless steel) rappel rings on the anchor. What goes around, comes around.

long time. But use your best judgment and retire anything you don't feel good about—webbing is cheap.

Abrasion is a much bigger concern with webbing because the load-bearing fibers are regularly exposed. A strong correlation exists between percentage of fuzzing and amount of strength loss. A study by one climbing company found that with 10 percent of the fibers cut, the webbing lost 20 percent of its strength, while cutting 30 percent of the fibers resulted in a 40 percent reduction.

Since nylon webbing doesn't have much, if any, water-repellent treatments, it will lose about 20 to 30 percent of its strength when soaking wet. If it has been exposed to a lot of sun, particularly at high altitudes, nylon webbing can lose as much as 37 percent of its original strength; around 15 percent is more typical, but it depends on color and degree of fading. Webbing made with HMPE is not affected by water or UV rays.

Rope Management

Among the most important skills for anyone who works with rope—be they climber, boater, arborist, caver, or whatever—is rope management. Few things lead to greater frustration and delay as a massively snarled "rope salad." Tangled ropes are the bane of our existence.

Ever notice how some people seem to turn any rope they touch into a hideous tangle while others, using the very same rope, seem immune to frustrating snarls? Watch them closely and it all boils down to proper rope management technique—a vital skill set, yet seldom taught or emphasized in schools or instructional books.

The "secret" of good rope management is paying attention. Keeping an ever vigilant eye out for potential problems will head most off beforehand. Of course, a lot can be said for learning from your mistakes too.

Remember: Thirty seconds of prevention saves thirty minutes of frustration!

STACKING

If you just toss a coil of rope down on the ground and start paying out one end, you will quickly end up with a massive mess in hand. In most cases, flaking the rope into a stack is far more time efficient.

While flaking a rope onto the ground seems a mindless thing, there should be a method to the madness. Start big, deliberately covering a large area, and finish small. This creates a rope pyramid that makes it less likely for loops to get entangled—the root of all evil. If using half or twin ropes, stack them together instead of making two piles; it makes management easier.

After you have lead a pitch and are belaying the second up, you will be taking in the rope and need to deal with it; plan ahead. If you are on a roomy ledge and will be swapping leads, simply make a pyramid as described earlier. Hanging belays on a steep face are fairly easy because you can just let the rope dangle.

Where things get tricky is at belays on small or sloping ledges and less than vertical hanging belays with cracks and flakes beneath that just love to eat ropes. This is when rope management requires serious attention or you will be in for a real headache belaying the leader up the next pitch. Indeed, stacking the rope properly in these situations is what separates good climbers from those who get benighted or caught by the storm—it's a major part of team efficiency.

The most common technique is to butterfly the rope across the tie-in (see Butterfly Coil, later in this chapter). This works best if the first loops are long and each successive loop is a tad shorter. You can also butterfly the rope over a foot or leg, but this basically means you can't move around without dropping the entire stack.

Another option for keeping a hanging belay tidy is to tie an over-hand loop loosely in the rope about every 40 feet and clip the loop to a carabiner (two or three loops per carabiner). This leaves a couple of 20-foot loops dangling and keeps the entire rope from snaking down under its own weight. Since the overhand does not resemble any load-bearing knot, you won't make the mistake of untying something critical. The belayer just needs to untie each loop a few feet before the slack is gone.

4.1 Rope Hook, for organizing belays

Perhaps the easiest method for rope management on multipitch climbs is to use a pair of Metolius Rope Hooks (each climber carries one). This simple, lightweight device provides a convenient place to hang a rope and saves having to coil and stack (photo 4.1). Of course, Luddites object to carrying an extra gizmo and homemade versions often don't work as well.

When managing multiple ropes on a big wall, rope buckets greatly simplify life; ropes stay organized and can be moved around easily. Essentially a funnel-shaped stuff sack with a carabiner loop, rope bags keep things organized but aren't worth carrying for normal rock climbs. Run the rope through a carabiner above the bucket so all you have to do is pull the rope straight in and stuff; it will feed out beautifully.

Block Organization

When a climbing team is not swinging leads, either because the second is not up for the next pitch or because you are climbing in blocks (the same climber leads several pitches in a row) for speed, then the rope stack must be rearranged. Otherwise, when the leader sets off again, the rope will feed from the bottom of the pile and a tangle is almost ensured.

There are three options: Each climber unties and ties into the opposite end (fast but risky); re-stack the entire rope (slower but safe); or prepare the rope to be rolled or flipped (fast but high potential for tangles). The first two options are self-explanatory, though be damned sure both of you are clipped in if you untie!

Rolling the rope so that the bottom is on top works best if you have carefully butterflied the rope over your tie-in. But, instead of starting with big loops and going smaller, make the first loops small and subsequent ones bigger. To transfer the rope to the second, run a shoulder-length sling under the rope and lift it off the tie-in. Clip the sling to an anchor or set the rope down across the second's tie-in. Then grasp the entire stack with both hands and rotate it so the small loops are on top. The rope should feed nicely.

Flipping the rope, as some climbers advocate, is fraught with peril of entanglement. The rope is butterflied as above, but the transfer is made by flipping the stack from the belayer/leader's tie-in to the follower/belayer's tie-in.

HEAVING

Whether heaving a dock line to a boat or tossing a rappel rope from a cliff top, opportunities abound for an instantaneous midair snafu. Many of us have seen it happen . . . as the rope leaves your hand, it miraculously transforms itself from neat coils into a snarled mass that comes up short, usually accompanied by a groan of dismay and frustration. The best method of heaving was figured out by sailors millennia ago but surprisingly few outdoorspeople have learned the technique.

In general, the goal when heaving rope is to get as much horizontal distance as possible and let gravity do the rest. Most snags occur from failure to get rappel ropes far enough away from the rock. Do not attempt to toss an entire climbing rope or you will be sorry. Never tie the bottom ends of rappel ropes together; this prevents a good toss and ensures kink-city by the time you reach the bottom. Use stopper knots and a rappel backup if you are not certain the ends reach the ground. This may sound obvious, but be sure the rope is anchored *before* you heave!

The following procedure is less complicated than it sounds and becomes even easier with practice. If you are right-handed, start at one end and butterfly about six loops onto the palm of your right hand. Make the loop on each side of your hand about 2 feet long (one arm's length) and be sure there are no twists. After six loops, extend your index and middle fingers and continue butterflying another six loops onto those two fingers so that the coil is divided in two (photo 4.2.A). Take the loops from your fingers into your left hand.

At this point, you have about six loops of rope in each hand. Look the loops over and make certain that they are neat and uncrossed (photo 4.2.B). Choose your trajectory, being mindful of trees and such. With an underhand swing, toss the coils in your right hand straight out (not downward) and leave your left hand wide open. The mass of tossed rope will cause the loops in the left hand to pay out smoothly before the toss uncoils; any remaining rope will be dragged down by the weight. The result: A clean, long-distance heave with no tangles!

This heaving method works well most of the time; however, in a

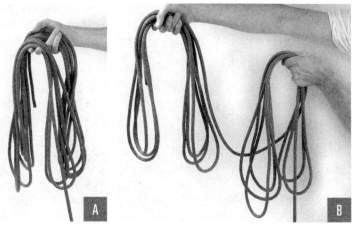

4.2 Heaving

strong wind it is better to modify things slightly. Toss the coils in the left hand while allowing those in the right to pay out but do not let go of the end (pinch between thumb and hand). This gets a big, heavy loop of rope below you and an outward flip of the end should help get it down the cliff.

Well, that's the theory anyhow. If the wind is blowing the ropes horizontal, the only good option is to rappel with them in a rope bag between you legs (best) or paying out of your pack (potential screw-ups). Another option is to lower the first climber, though communication becomes a problem without radios.

This technique works well for rigging climbing and caving ropes to rappel. But if you need to get a heavier line across a gap or get a rope up into a tree, you will need to use a heaving line. This is just a thin, strong cord with a heavy weight attached; it is tossed and then used to pull the heavy rope.

A point of courtesy when rigging rappels and top ropes: Do not shout "Rope!" as you have make the toss—it's already too late. Instead, give a shout and wait about ten seconds to give those below time to respond or scramble out of the way.

COILING & RACKING

It is a little-known fact that ropes are living creatures. If you make a pile of rope and watch out of the corner of your eye, you can sometimes see the unique mating process in which loops intertwine all on their own. Ropes are shy, so you will never see this copulation if you stare straight at the heap.

To prevent inbreeding and the nasty results, carefully manage ropes by proper coiling. Unfortunately, if you aren't careful, ropes can still find ways to create mischief. You can manage shorter loops of cord and webbing by "racking" them into a small package that is less prone to snagging.

As you will see in Chapter 5, names cause a great deal of confusion. This is equally a problem when the subject is coiling ropes. Thanks to authors of various how-to books using conflicting terms, you can't just say "use a mountaineer's coil" or "make a lap coil" and expect anyone to know what you mean.

Coiling Basics

Typically, people think of coiling as making a collection of successive circles. If the coil is carefully created and unwound, the rope will run true. However, inattention to detail can result in a massively kinked rope.

The alternative method is to butterfly the rope by forming loops alternating on either side of the hand. This is not only faster but also eliminates twisting problems. There is also less chance of snarling because there are half the number of circles as in a traditional coil.

Coils formed by either method need some wraps of rope to bind them together; these in turn need to be secured with a finishing knot. On a sailboat at sea, however, coils must be ready for fast deployment, so they are usually hung from a cleat and bound only when the boat is docked.

Often a rope is attached to a solid object ("made fast," in sailing terms) and the excess needs to be neatly stored. Always start coiling from the anchor point and work toward the end. This forces kinks and twists off the rope instead of trapping them in the middle.

When coiling a laid rope, always coil in a counterclockwise direction, which is the direction of the twist. It is unlikely you will encounter a rope with a clockwise twist, although they do exist. By coiling with the twist, you ensure the rope stays wound up.

SKEIN COIL

A skein coil is probably the most common coiling method for utility ropes; it is what many people use for an electric extension cord. When you purchase a new climbing or caving rope, it most likely will come in a skein coil (pronounced like "stain" but with a "k" instead of "t").

Advantages
Fast and easy.

Disadvantages
Works well only with short to moderate rope lengths (about 20 to 100 feet) unless you use a skein winder. Can impart twists into the rope.

Technique
Grasp one end of the rope. Wind the rope around your elbow and palm (photo 4.3.A). Finish off with a couple of wraps around the center and tuck the end of the rope through the loops (photo 4.3.B).

Variations
You can improvise a skein winder from a variety of objects: the legs of a bar stool, a stiff piece of cardboard, a coffee can, your palm. Some objects you leave in place for storing the rope; others you re-

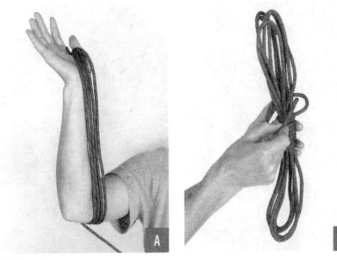

4.3 Skein Coil

move after coiling. Base the size of the object on the rope diameter and length.

CLIMBER'S COIL

This is the traditional method of coiling a climbing rope. It is presented here mostly as an example of what *not* to do, to clear up naming confusion, and as a bit of nostalgia for the geezers. Back when I was climbing on Goldline ropes, this was our sole coiling method. But I quit using it on climbing ropes two decades ago. The climber's coil does work nicely for short lengths (under 100 feet) of utility rope.

Other Names
Alpine coil
Lap coil
Mountaineer's coil
Standing coil

Advantages
A properly tied climber's coil is a work of art, partly because it takes so much work to do it right. It's the proper coil for posing in wool knickers with a wooden ice axe. The big circle does strap nicely to the outside of a pack.

If your partner sprains an ankle and can't walk, you can improvise

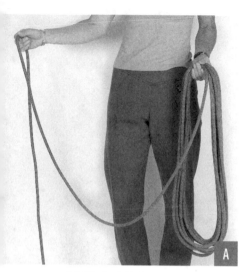 

4.4 Climber's Coil

a handy carrying harness from a climber's coil. Split the coil to create two circles on either side of the lashing (looks like a big butterfly). Have the victim place a leg in each circle, get in front of them, and use the circles as shoulder straps. Enjoy the hump, hero.

If you are ever a deckhand on a boat, you'll need to know how to properly "coil down a cable."

Disadvantages
Slow to coil, slow to uncoil—fast to kink, tangle, and frustrate.

Technique
Hold one end, leaving about two feet of rope hanging down. If you are using your right hand, have the end toward you; if using your left, hold it away from you. Using your free hand, begin making loops in a clockwise direction. As you bring each loop up, roll the rope in your fingers to give it a half twist toward the coil. If you get this rotation right, you'll have an even circle hanging straight down (photo 4.4.A). Failure to roll the rope, or rolling in the wrong direction, will yield a giant figure eight.

With a bit of practice, you can get a rhythm going. Keeping your arm straight (the one holding the circle of coils), let it pendulum from the shoulder. As you swing the coils away, the weight pulls a full arm's length of rope into the other hand. As you swing the circle of coils

back, the hand adds another coil. It's actually pretty fast once you figure it out.

As you add more coils to your hand, you may need to change the half twist to a full twist or even multiple twists to get the whole loop hanging straight. The rope at your feet will accumulate more and more twists; migrate these toward the end with vigorous up and down flicking.

After the entire rope is coiled, take the starting end and make a bight (a tight fold) (photo 4.4.B). Wrap the finishing end about six times around the rope coils, toward the bight, and the bight. Tuck the end through the bight and pull the starting end snug (photo 4.4.C).

Variations

Some climbers merely wrap the rope around foot and knee (or both feet and knees). This is faster but the circles will turn out as figure eights since the rope doesn't get a twist with each coil. You can also make the loops over your head instead of in hand, but that won't yield neat coils either.

To prevent snags while crawling, cavers spiral the end of the rope around the entire circumference of the coil, making turns about four inches apart, before adding the finishing knot. For that I have two words: rope bags. The only reason for a caver's coil these days is to make a wall display with an alpenstock and hob-nailed boots.

BUTTERFLY COIL

The surprising thing about the butterfly coil is that it took so long to become widely accepted. At first it was used only among climbers as an easy way to carry the rope when scrambling; the butterfly coil wasn't even described in instructional books until the 1980s. Eventually, the many other benefits became apparent and it took over at the crags.

Because it is fast and does not create kinks, the butterfly coil is the method of choice for most ropes—especially longer ones. The technique is easy to master and there are good variations for those with small hands or weak arms.

A butterflied rope is less likely to tangle than a coiled rope because there are half as many circles (two lobes of a butterfly make one circle) that are twice as big.

Other Names
Alpine coil
Backpack coil
Lap coil
Mountaineer's coil
Pack coil

Advantages
Fast and friendly. Does not twist a rope. Works with ropes of any length. Less prone to tangles.

Disadvantages
Starting with both ends in hand means the rope must always be stacked before use. The pendulum trick described in the climber's coil doesn't work as well because one lobe tends to snag.

4.5 Butterfly Coil, Technique #1, Hand Method

Technique #1

Hand Method: Start either with both ends of the rope or with the center mark in one hand. Extend the arm outward to measure out a span of rope, using the opposite hand as a guide for the two strands. Bring the guide hand up to the holding hand and lay the strands across your palm in alternating directions so that loops form on either side (photo 4.5.A). Continue until the entire rope is butterflied.

Locate the two ends that are next to each other in the stack. Drop off three loops, so about 15 feet (4.5 meters) of rope lies on the ground (drop only two loops if the rope is going into a pack). Make two to four wraps upward around all the loops and pull snug (photo 4.5.B). Bring the two strands up to the holding hand and place them in the fingers. Now, by pulling your holding hand back, bring a large bight through (photo 4.5.C). Poke the strands through the bight, making a girth hitch, take up the slack, and give a good shake.

If you will be wearing the rope, the strands should be around 5 to 6 feet (1.5 meters) long. Swing the rope around to your back and run a strand over each shoulder. Bring the strands under your arms and cross them around the rope, switching hands behind your back. Slide your hands out the new strands and tie a square knot in front (photo 4.5.D). Strands that are too long can be tucked away or you can undo the

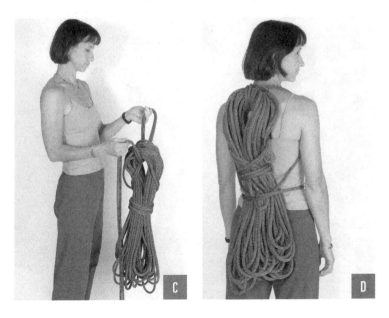

finishing knot and add one more wrap. Wear the rope high between your shoulder blades so that loops do not tangle and catch on bushes.

Uncoil a butterflied rope by undoing the fastening knot. Some will meticulously flake a double coiled rope onto the ground and then restack it into a proper pile. But usually you can just set the coils down and stack the rope, gently removing the few tangles that may occur. It's almost always best to take the time to flake out a single coiled rope. Always start stacking by tossing the end well off to the side so you won't have to hunt for it under the pile.

Technique #2

Neck Method: No doubt, 200 feet of 10.5-mm is a lot of rope. It can be a serious workout to hand coil that much, especially if you are already pumped from climbing. And some people can't hold that many strands in their hand. The solution is neck coiling, described here as a single coil although the rope can also be doubled.

Hang the rope around your neck with the end about hip level on your left side. Pinch the rope with the right hand at the same level. Grab the rope with your left hand and raise it up over your head to make a loop. Drop your left hand and pinch the new strand and cast the rope around your neck with the right hand (photo 4.6.A). Repeat

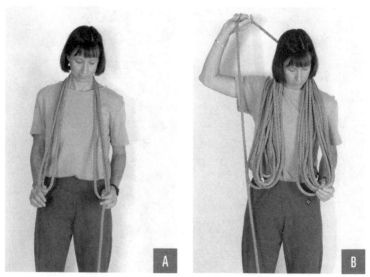

4.6 Butterfly Coil, Technique #2, Neck Method

until the entire rope is hanging neatly butterflied around your neck (photo 4.6.B). With a little practice, you can pick up the speed and look like a whirling Dervish. Duck your head and lift the rope off with either hand.

If a rope will be carried under the lid of a pack, you don't want long strands dangling or unraveling. Uncoil the last two loops and use this length to make about five wraps around the center of the coil, leaving an arm span of rope. Snug it all up and make one wrap in the same direction around half the strands. Poke the end through the center loop and bring it around the other half of the strands. Tuck the end under the last two loops formed and pull everything tight.

Variations

When exploring canyons and caves, it's sometimes necessary to negotiate many short drops with only one or two long rappels. It's a waste of time to coil and uncoil the full length of a rope for a 20-foot rappel. Instead, coil the rope in halves, or even one-third/two-thirds.

Match one end to the center mark on the rope. Butterfly the doubled rope into your hand but make the loops about half the size as normal. When the rope is coiled to the center mark and end, back off so the tail is about a full arm span long. Finish off with two full wraps and a girth hitch as you would for a butterfly coil.

The final step is to pull the bight of the girth hitch through until it is large enough to slip over the head of the coil. Work all the new loops down and you end up with a single strand emerging from the rope coil (variously called a buntline or gasket coil). Repeat the entire procedure on the other half of the rope and you get two butterfly coils connected by a single strand that you can wear around your neck.

CHAIN STITCH

This is a fast way to keep rope snakes at bay. It is particularly useful prior to washing a rope in a laundry machine so you don't end up with the tangle from hell. But it is also a handy way of reducing trip or tangle potential while still allowing fast deployment; parachutists use it to keep lines from fouling.

Other Names
Electrician's braid
Double monkey chain

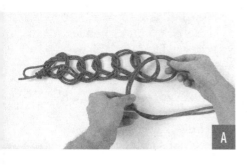

4.7 *Chain Stitch*

Technique

A chain stitch is essentially a string of slip knots. If chaining a loop, start at the knot or stitching and make a slip knot so that the bulk jams. (For washing a rope, first tie an overhand loop at the center; this will keep the coils more secure during the washer agitation.) Reach through the eye with the fingers of your right hand and pull a bight through, making it several inches long (photo 4.7.A). Repeat through each successive new bight until you reach the end. Pinching the growing chain between your knees gives something to pull against, speeding the process. Finish off a chained loop by poking the end through the final double-strand bight and pulling (photo 4.7.B). Finish a chained rope by sticking the two ends through the last loop and pulling the girth hitch tight.

CORDELETTE RACK

Long runners of accessory cord—called cordelettes—have a multitude of uses for climbers. Frequently, when a quick anchor point is needed, a giant runner is the most expedient answer (for more details, see Anchors, Chapter 7). Cordelettes are made from about a 20-foot (6-meter) length of 5-mm high-strength (aramid or HMPE core) or 7-mm nylon cord tied into a loop with a double or triple fisherman's bend.

Climbers normally carry a cordelette clipped to the back of the sit harness, so it's out of the way until needed at belays. Handy tool, but cordelettes can be a nuisance if not racked properly. Following are a couple methods for turning cordelettes into tidy, snag-proof bundles.

Technique #1

Twist Method: The first step is to reduce the cordelette to between 12 and 16 inches (30 to 40 cm); the specifics depend upon the starting size and whether you want long and skinny or short and fat (photo 4.8.A). For some cordelettes, you can first halve the loop and then halve it again, possibly even halving it a third time. If that doesn't achieve the desired size, make two loops in the cordelette, put a finger of each hand inside, and pull apart. This divides the cordelette into thirds, which you then halve.

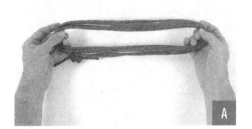

Once you've condensed the cordelette, put one or two fingers of each hand inside and twist the entire collection of loops tightly (two to five turns) (photo 4.8.B). Bring both fingers together and pinch one finger and thumb through all the loops. Clip a carabiner next to your fingers and give a tug and twist to set everything (photo 4.8.C).

4.8 Cordelette Rack, Technique #1, Twist Method

Technique #2

Coil Method: For a more compact package with even less snag potential, take a few extra seconds for this method. Halve the cordelette, then halve it again to create four loops about 14 to 20 inches (35 to 55 cm) long dangling from one thumb.

Take a loop without the fisherman's bend and let it dangle; you now have two small loops and one long one. Give a twist to the small loops (creating a figure eight) and bring the bottom part of the figure eight up to your thumb. You now have four small loops and one big one. Repeat one more time so you have eight small loops (about 6 inches, or 15 cm, long), plus the one big loop (roughly 46 inches, or 115 cm, long) (photo 4.9.A).

Now wrap the big loop snugly around all the small loops, starting at the bottom and spiraling upward (photo 4.9.B). When it's snug, poke the tip of the big loop through the group of small loops, next to your thumb. Snug it all up and clip a carabiner into the single loop (photo 4.9.C). You have a tidy package.

SLING RACK

It is a good idea for climbers to carry several readily accessible, 18-inch-long (45 cm) loops made of 6-mm nylon accessory cord. Often called Prusik slings, these are used for back-

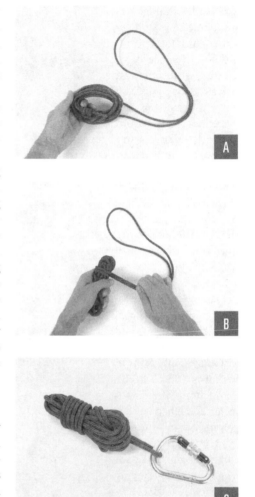

4.9 Cordelette Rack, Technique #2, Coil Method

ing up a rappel or escaping a belay in an emergency. They are also handy for many rescue situations, such as extricating someone from a crevasse. However, Prusik slings can be troublesome if not racked properly. If you simply condense each sling into short loops, one invariably snags on something and you end up with one long, dangling loop. Here is a simple method for carrying Prusik slings; it will prevent them from snagging and it is easy to unfurl.

Technique

Put a finger of each hand in the sling and pull your hands apart, offsetting the knot so it's at one end and to the side. Fold about a quarter of the loop over your finger and toward the middle (photo 4.10.A). Now start wrapping the long part of the loop around the short part; try to keep the strands neat but don't worry too much (photo 4.10.B). Clip a carabiner through the ends of both loops and give it all a twist to tidy it; sometimes you have to rotate a loop to get everything to set together (photo 4.10.C). The tension holds the structure together. For fast, one-handed deployment, simply unclip one of the loops and shake out the sling.

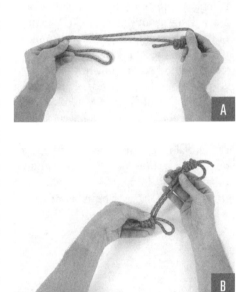

4.10 Sling Rack

UNSNARLING

Snarls happen. Despite your best efforts, the gremlins inevitably will make their appearance. The key is to deal with the issue early, when it is easier to solve.

Nearly all rope salads are merely loops within loops. Find the right loops and the puzzle quickly unravels. The one thing you absolutely should not do is blindly pull an end of the rope out of the heap—this can create a knot of biblical proportions! Don't go jerking wildly either, or you'll just tighten up loops and make your job harder.

If an entire coil of rope has become snarled, one tedious but effective method is to start by loosening everything up. Then locate where the longest end enters the heap and gently open a hole around it, creating a donut. Your mission is to keep unrolling the entire tangle away from the free strand, repeatedly turning the donut inside out. Do not pull hard on the strand or you will just complicate matters. If the unrolling method seems hopeless, carefully push a strand into the pile and pull it out the other side. Continue pushing a strand in and pulling it through until the rope comes unsnarled.

Stay calm: These things have a way of happening at the most inopportune times. If you are in the middle of a rappel and spy a tangle or potential jam in the rope below you, stop (either with your backup knot or a leg wrap), pull the problem up to you, and deal with it. Do not rappel past a snagged or jammed end of the rope and expect to fix things; it is rarely better from below.

Knot Basics

A friend once teased, "How hard can knots be? I mean, there is the square knot, the thingamajig knot, the 'I can't remember how to tie this so I'll just loop this around this and pass through this and pray' knot and a 'granny junker' after that . . . what else do you really need?" While he is a very experienced outdoorsperson, this sentiment is shared by many who never learned—or were improperly taught—the basics of knotting.

At the opposite extreme are the "knot obsessed" knotters who can rattle off names of obscure knots tied by herdsmen on the Siberian steppes, gardeners in Japan, and sailors on whaling ships. They might belong to the International Guild of Knot Tyers and may even compete in speed tying contests. The godfather of knots, Clifford Ashley, who wrote the bible, *The Ashley Book of Knots,* stated, "To me the simple act of tying a knot is an adventure in unlimited space."

Unfortunately, the well-meaning second group tends to confuse the heck out of the first group—often to the point that those in the first group resort to the granny junker knot for everything. Many knot books are so intimidating that they scare off even avid knot users.

While I've certainly tied my share of thingamajig knots, and played with many of the fancy versions, I've settled on a basic repertoire of knots that, used alone or combined, can handle anything necessary in the outdoors. Less is more. Keep it simple.

KNOT TERMINOLOGY

In biology, the wide variety of common names led to the development of a standardized naming system (using Latin) to avoid confusion.

Alas, we have no equivalent for knots.

Part of the confusion about knots arises from the terminology knotters use. A "bend" sounds like "the rope ain't straight." Tell the average person to grab the "standing part of the rope," and he or she will look at you quizzically, thinking, "I'm not standing on the rope."

Where things really get convoluted is with the names of knots, some of which have existed since before the written word. Traditions in different cultures have led to various names for the same knot. Sometimes a person's name is incorrectly attributed to a knot (for example, the Munter hitch). In other cases, a knot is misnamed but the usage has become so widespread that it is commonly accepted (for example, the Prusik is a hitch but is often called a knot).

Rope Parts

A lot of people think a rope has just three parts: two ends and a middle. But for the purpose of discussing knots, we need to be more specific. What you do with those ends and the middle makes a big difference.

Bight: When you double the rope back on itself, with the strands parallel and close together, you have a "bight." A knot may be tied *with* a bight instead of a single strand of rope. Or a knot may tied *in* a bight, which means that it is tied along the length of the rope without using an end.

Loop: If you take the bight and twist it, the strands cross and you now have what most people call a "loop" (knotters call it a "crossing turn"). At various times, the distinction between a bight and a loop becomes important.

Standing Part: This is the remainder of the rope hanging from, or on the opposite side of, the knot from the "working end."

Tail: When you tie a knot near the end of a rope, the short end left over, dangling from one side, is called the "tail." Often the tail is purposely left long to serve as a grab handle or as insurance against the knot pulling apart.

Working End: The part of the rope you hold in your hand is the "working end," or simply the "end."

Knotting Terms

Where possible, I have avoided using confusing terminology and tried to stick with plain language. However, some terms are required for clarity. Other words may be encountered in other texts, so it's worth knowing what they mean even if you don't use them.

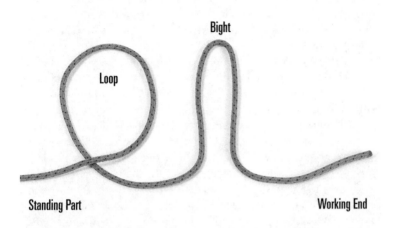

5.1 Parts of the rope

Bend: A "bend" is created when two ropes, or the ends of the same rope, are joined together.

Capsize: Some knots will "capsize" to form another knot when loaded in unusual directions.

Dressed: When some knots, such as the figure-eight loop, are first tied, often the strands are crossed and do not lie neatly against each other—if loaded, this sloppy knot can be significantly weaker than planned. The penultimate step in finishing any knot is to properly "dress" it. This means to take a moment and tidy the knot.

Flake: For climbers, to "flake" a rope means to uncoil it by peeling layers off the coil one at a time into a stack on the ground. (It has the opposite meaning for sailors; the rope is coiled.) This reduces the odds of a tangle as the rope is paid out.

Frapping: The finishing wraps made around a lashing that binds two poles. Frapping turns pull the lashing tight.

Hitch: When fastening a rope to a fixed object (tree, carabiner, even another rope), you are using a "hitch." Some hitches, such as the clove hitch, are fixed and anchor the rope in place. Others, such as the Munter hitch, are sliding hitches used to control the line. Yet others, such as the Prusik and Bachmann, are friction hitches that slide up a rope or pole but grab when the loop is pulled.

Knot: In proper knot-speak, a "knot" is a formed when two parts of the same rope are purposefully twisted or intertwined. When you tie your shoes, that's a knot. (In bird-speak, a knot is a small sandpiper, *Calidris canutus*.)

Set: After the knot has been dressed, all the parts need to be pulled tight. This "set" ensures that the knot performs in a predictable manner. A good knot is said to be "properly dressed and set."

Spill: A knot often "spills" when it unties accidentally. For example, a square knot can spill into a girth hitch that will slip off the end of the rope. The square knot can also be spilled on purpose to untie it.

Splice: The other way to join laid (and some braided) ropes is by "splicing" them, which means to unravel the working ends and then braid them together. A good splice is nearly as strong (90 to 95 percent) as the weaker rope; the ropes don't have to be the same diameter or even material (rope can be spliced to steel cable). Splices are handy for smoothly, and permanently, joining ropes used on sailboats or for making a neat eye in one end. However, I've never had to use a splice for outdoor activities and will not include any in this book.

Turn: Take a strand of rope and wrap it around an object so that both ends point in the same direction. You've just made a "turn." Take that same piece of rope and wrap it once around the object, making one and a half circles, so both ends are pointed in the same direction. You now have a "round turn." Encircle the object a few more times and you have "multiple turns."

Whipping: This is a fancy way to keep the ends of a rope from unraveling or to mark distance along a rope. To "whip" a rope, wrap a string around it and draw the string up tight. This gives the rope a nautical look but isn't necessarily better than just wrapping with tape and melting the ends thoroughly. On climbing ropes, a whipped middle mark does not feed well through a belay device, so it can be a nuisance when belaying and on rappels.

KNOT STRENGTHS

A rope is strongest when it is straight. Anything you do that puts curves in the rope will weaken it. The tighter the curve, the weaker the rope.

The reason for this strength loss is pretty simple when you think about it. In a straight rope, all the forces are equally aligned, so all the fibers share the load. A curve or pinch in the rope or webbing strains the fibers on the outside and compresses the fibers on the inside, so that the inside and outside fibers are no longer working together.

KNOT STRENGTHS

Testing knots until they break is fun. You get to use powerful machines and pull things apart until something explodes. However, it's also time-consuming and expensive to do right since you need enough samples to get statistically valid figures. Furthermore, the results can vary widely depending upon the ropes or webbing used, how the knot was tied and dressed, and the method of testing. No standards exist for testing knots.

All of these variables make it difficult to get reliable strength figures, so don't accept ratings on blind faith. The numbers that follow were derived from many sources and are certainly open to interpretation and debate. When it comes to determining how much strength loss results from a particular knot, there are no absolutes.

Straight Rope	100 percent
Loop Knots	
Bowline	55 – 74 percent
Butterfly	61 – 72 percent
Overhand Loop	58 – 68 percent
Figure-Eight Loop	66 – 77 percent
Figure-Nine Loop	68 – 84 percent
Double Figure-Eight Loop	61 – 77 percent
Joining Knots	
Double Fisherman's	65 – 80 percent
Water Knot (in webbing)	60 – 70 percent
Figure-Eight Bend	70 – 75 percent
Square Knot	43 – 47 percent
Fastening Knots[1]	
Clove Hitch	60 – 75 percent
Two Half Hitches	60 – 75 percent
Girth Hitch	40 – 75 percent
Timber Hitch	65 – 70 percent

[1]The diameter of the object directly affects the knot's strength.

Thus, all other things being equal, knots with a larger radius are typically stronger than small-radius knots. Similarly, a rope passing around a large tree trunk is stronger than a rope going through a carabiner.

Before we get too far into the knot-strength discussion, consider this: No climbers have ever been injured or killed because their tie-in knot broke. Unfortunately, numerous serious injuries and deaths can be attributed to poorly tied knots. Don't sweat the strength issue for tying a rope to your harness, just remember to finish whichever knot you choose! Stop talking for the few seconds it takes and stay focused on staying alive.

WHEN NOT TO KNOT

There is a time and a place for everything. And sometimes there are better alternatives to knots.

As mentioned in Chapter 2, Rope Selection, most webbing that is made with HMPE is too slick to hold a standard knot. This material is sold only as sewn runners or attached to climbing cams. If the webbing becomes so fuzzed from abrasion that it needs replacement, retire the runners and send the cams in to a specialist for new slings.

Several friction hitches are described in this book and every climber should have a couple of them in their bag of tricks—these are essential in emergencies for escaping a belay, assisting injured climbers, and retrieving dropped gear. However, if you are planning on ascending fixed lines, do yourself a favor and take mechanical ascenders. It really is no fun using knots to climb two hundred feet while dangling in mid-air.

For rigging the guylines on a tent, the tautline hitch works fairly well and is valuable to know. But the newer plastic line tensioners are even easier to use, particularly when the guylines are wet or frozen. The nicest of these have three holes with two that open on the side so they can be quickly removed or added to the tent.

For tying canoes or rafts onto a vehicle, the trucker's hitch is handy at times. But anyone who spends much time on the river should purchase an assortment of webbing straps with aluminum camlock buckles. These are so much easier than tying a knot and you can haul down on them pretty hard. Cam straps are also great for lashing gear in boats. Take note that the buckles range in quality; some are rated to 400 lbf (1.8 kN) while others hold 1,200 lbf (5.4 kN).

Chapter
6

Knots for Hiking & Camping

Over the centuries, innumerable knots have been developed for a wide variety of purposes. *The Ashley Book of Knots,* one of the most complete references, took eleven years to compile, contains several hundred knots (not the oft-quoted thousands), and still only scratches the surface.

Yet out of this plethora of knots, just a handful need to be in the repertoire of outdoorspeople. If you take the time to really learn the first ten knots in this chapter, you will be prepared to handle about 90 percent of the situations encountered when hiking and camping.

The ten essential knots also form the foundation for many of the more specialized knots used by climbers and paddlers. Do not proceed to Chapter 7 or 8 without mastering these.

The remaining five knots in this chapter fall in the good-to-know category. The Prusik and timber hitch are so easy to learn that you may as well add them to the memory banks; odds are you will use them someday. Building temporary structures, such as lean-tos or corrals, isn't something most of us will do often, but the skill could be handy. And knowing how to lash logs could help you build an emergency stretcher or a footbridge over a raging creek.

SLIP KNOT

As the name implies, this is a noose knot that slips away when one end is pulled. There are countless uses for a slip knot, from tying off lines temporarily or quickly adding a stopper on a rope to making a locking hitch with a runner. The slip knot is also the starting point for other knots, including the bowline, and the ending point for yet others, such as the shoelace knot.

Other Names
Overhand slipknot
Overhand knot with draw loop
Slipped overhand
Noose knot

Advantages
It slips. Excellent for temporary fastening. Can be used to create a pulley for tensioning a rope (see Trucker's Hitch, Chapter 8) or tent guyline. Tied in succession, slip knots can keep a rope tidy but quickly deployable (see Chain Stitch, Chapter 4). When a slip knot is made in a runner, it will cinch around protruding objects (such as a piton, ice screw, or rock horn) to hold the runner in place.

Disadvantages
It slips. This one-sided knot falls apart when the wrong strand is pulled, so be sure to anticipate which strand will receive the load. The loop tends to snag on things when used as a stopper knot.

Technique
Make a loop in the rope. Choose the strand that will slip and make a bight (photo 6.1.A). Pass the bight through the loop. Put a finger through the bight and grab the two rope strands with the other hand. Draw up the knot snug by pulling your hands apart (photo 6.1.B).

If you are near the end of the rope, just tie

6.1 Slip Knot

an overhand and stick the end back through the hole.

For temporarily tying off to an anchor point such as a tree or ring with a very long rope, pass a long bight around or through the anchor and tie a slip knot with the bight around the rope. Snug this up firmly with the end of the bight near the knot. Use the two long loops to make a half hitch around the rope for extra security. (Also see Mooring Hitch, Chapter 8.)

Variation

Slipped Slipknot: Sometimes when you are tying off with a stiff rope to a small or smooth round object, a slip knot will not grab. And other times, a plain slip knot sets too tight and is difficult to release. This just takes a simple modification.

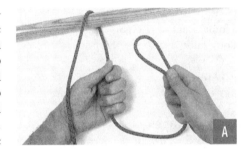

Pass the rope around the object with the load-bearing portion on the left side. Make a bight in the rope on the right side with your right hand. Reach under the loaded line with the left hand and grab the working rope above the bight (photo 6.2.A). Pull your left hand back and rotate the wrist to make a loop (photo 6.2.B). Now tuck the bight in your right hand over the loaded line and through the loop. Tension the loaded line to snug it all up to the object (photo 6.2.C).

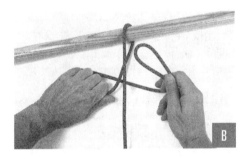

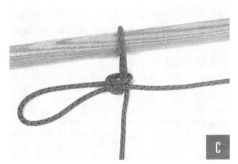

6.2 Slipped Slipknot

OVERHAND LOOP

They don't get much simpler—or handier—than this. Whenever you need a quick loop that doesn't have to take much weight, the overhand is a good choice. It's also ideal when you want permanent loops in a rope that will be loaded, such as a handline on a slippery slope.

6.3 Overhand Loop

Other Names
Thumb knot on a bight
Loop knot

Advantages
Faster than a speeding bullet. Secure even in shock cord.

Disadvantages
Once loaded, it will take much cursing—and perhaps a marlinespike—to untie.

Technique
Make a bight. Pass it over both strands and around to the back. Poke the bight through the hole. Snug (photo 6.3).

FIGURE-EIGHT LOOP

What a difference a half-turn makes! The mere act of continuing around to the front transforms the overhand loop into the figure-eight loop, which surely belongs in the pantheon of knots. This beautifully symmetrical knot is among the strongest due to the large radius of the bends. After it has been pulled taut, the figure-eight loop is easier to undo from kernmantle ropes than an overhand loop.

Other Names
Figure-eight on a bight
Flemish loop

Advantages
Strong and reliable. Simple to tie and easy to check visually. Adequate even when improperly dressed.

Disadvantages

This is a unidirectional knot that works best when the pull is aligned with the rope. Although some texts recommend the figure-eight loop for isolating a damaged section of rope, it is a poor choice due to the geometry. Use a butterfly loop (Chapter 7) when the load comes from multiple directions or the strands are pulled apart. The inline figure-eight loop (Chapter 7) is better when the eye is pulled parallel to the rope.

Difficult to untie, particularly when wet, so mariners have traditionally avoided it.

Technique

Make a bight in the rope. Pass it over both strands, then around to the back and continue around the strands to the front (photo 6.4.A). Poke the bight through the hole (photo 6.4.B). Snug.

Although easy to tie, the figure-eight loop is deceptively tricky to dress. Even when you think you have it right, closer inspection often reveals crossing strands. While an undressed knot will do the job, it can be harder to untie afterward and is likely weaker.

Often you can "break" a tightened figure eight by flexing it back and forth in the middle, which works a bit more rope into the knot. Also try shoving rope into the knot while pushing against the loops at that end with your thumb. Silent cursing can help relieve tension.

Variations

Figure-Nine: To make the knot even stronger, but bulkier, simply make one more half-turn around the strands. The resulting figure-nine loop is easier to untie after significant loading, so it is common in rescue applications.

6.4 Figure-Eight Loop

The figure nine may also be used to join two ropes (see Figure-Nine Bend, Chaper 7).

Double Loop Figure-Eight: Sometimes it is useful to have two loops instead of one. Start with a regular figure-eight loop but make the bight extra long. Instead of poking the entire bight through the knot, just fold it in half and stick that through (like making a slip knot). Now flip the single loop over the double loops and slide it up past the knot. Pull the double loops and dress. (Doing this is faster than reading about it.)

If you need three loops, bring the single loop around the two rope strands and poke it through the same hole as the double loops. While very fast and strong, the double and triple figure-eight loops are rather difficult to adjust. (For an easier two-loop knot, see Bowline-on-a-Bight, Chapter 7.)

SQUARE KNOT

A prehistoric knot that was advocated for binding wounds 2,000 years ago and more recently used for reefing sails on square-riggers, the square knot is elegant and, when used appropriately, strong enough for light duty.

Other Names
Reef knot

Advantages
Good, easy knot for binding. Use it for such tasks as tying packages, holding bundles, or making wound dressings.

Disadvantages
Among the weakest of knots that join two ropes, yielding only about 45 percent of tensile strength. It can jam tight, making it difficult to untie. When load is applied to only one rope (standing part and tail are pulled apart), the knot capsizes into a girth hitch and the other rope will slip off the end.

Technique
Right over left, left over right.

Grab one rope in each hand and cross the strand in your right hand over the left strand (photo 6.5.A). Wrap the top strand around the other (photo 6.5.B). Now cross the new left strand over the new right strand and through the hole (photo 6.5.C). Snug.

The square knot is always perfectly symmetrical, with the strands

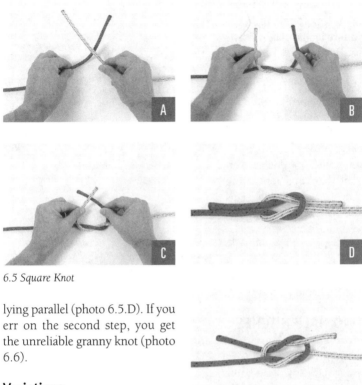

6.5 Square Knot

lying parallel (photo 6.5.D). If you err on the second step, you get the unreliable granny knot (photo 6.6).

Variations

Shoelace Knot: Most people learn to tie their shoes by tying an overhand, making a bight in one end and tying a slip knot around

6.6 Unreliable Granny Knot

it with the other to form the bow. If your laces often come untied, you've probably been tying a granny instead of a square knot; it's a common mistake. Find out which knot you use by pulling the loops through and examining the knot. Those who learned the granny simply need to reverse the first step (i.e., if you usually start right over left, switch to left over right); the bows will be perpendicular to your foot, not parallel. For greater security, tie the overhand, then make a bight in both ends and use these to complete the square knot.

One-Way Square Bend: If a rope will be pulled through a confined space, avoid jams by having the tails point backward. After tying a square knot, take the tail of the pulling line over and around the line (photo 6.7.A) and back through its own loop between the strands of the other rope (this makes a figure eight) (photo 6.7.B).

Square Fisherman's: This is a square knot backed up on each side with a double overhand knot (photo 6.8). Some texts advocate this knot for joining two climbing ropes. However, the safety of this rigmarole depends upon the double overhand backups remaining tied, so set them tight. This knot is also more prone to jamming in cracks. It works, but there are better alternatives, such as the offset overhand bend and figure-nine bend (Chapter 7).

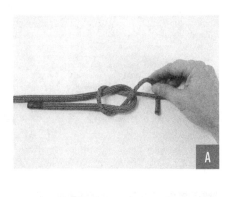

TWO HALF HITCHES

Ah, sweet simplicity! Humans probably figured out this knot soon after crawling down from the trees. It's a great way to tie off a tent guyline, secure a rope to a tree, or moor a boat.

6.7 One-Way Square Bend

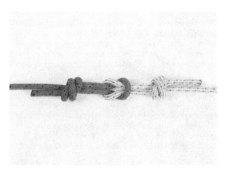

Other Names
Double half hitch

Advantages

6.8 Square Fisherman's

Super fast, super easy, reasonably secure, and easy to untie. Can be tied when the rope is under tension.

Disadvantages
Can be a nuisance to untie if you don't do a round turn. A third half hitch may be necessary with some ropes for security.

Technique

Pass the rope end behind the object (post, tree, whatever), then take the end and pass it around the rope and poke the end up through the hole (photo 6.9.A). Repeat one more time, continuing in the same direction with the end just below the first half hitch, and cinch it all up (photo 6.9.B). To take some strain off the knot, thereby increasing security, make a complete pass around the anchor (a "round turn") before tying the half hitches.

If you examine the two half hitches, you will see they form a clove hitch around the rope (photo 6.9.C). When the direction of the second hitch is reversed, the result is a girth hitch around the rope; this is far less secure.

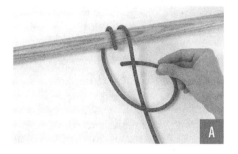

6.9 Two Half Hitches

Variation
Slipped Half Hitches:
Make the first hitch a slip knot and use the loop to make a half hitch around the rope to lock it (photo 6.10). This is easy to untie when it's time to move on.

CLOVE HITCH

This is among the most useful ways of securing a rope to an anchor point. It is very easy to adjust

6.10 Slipped Half Hitches

and usually can be loosened easily. The clove hitch is invaluable for climbers and sailors, but just about anyone who spends time in the outdoors will use it at some point.

Once snug, the clove hitch can be quite strong and will self-tighten as the load increases. However, the diameter of the anchor makes a big difference: bigger is better. With standard climbing rope, a clove can slip in a carabiner at high loads (around 1,000 lbf, 4.5 kN), which can help equalize anchor points and reduce impact forces at a belay station when things go really wrong. Stiff ropes may slip at considerably lower loads.

Although the clove hitch is a simple knot, I have watched many people struggle figuring it out . . . and have had my own share of mental moments.

Advantages
Great way to attach a rope to a tree, post, ring, or darn near anything cylindrical. Handy knot for binding the mouth of a sack. Superb for rigging belays on climbs because of the ease of adjustment. Secure when only one strand is loaded.

Disadvantages
The clove hitch is less secure when tied around a rectangular or square object or if the rope is very stiff. And it can loosen with repeated small tugs, such as from a canoe rocking in the water. In those situations, use a round turn with two half hitches. When the rope is wet, it can be very tough to untie a tightened clove hitch.

If it isn't pulled tight, the clove hitch can ride up and open the gate of a carabiner; locking carabiners are best. Never rely on a single clove hitch as a life point. One anchor in a belay should have a loop knot.

Technique #1
Finger Twirl: When attaching a clove to a carabiner or over a post, it is often easiest to tie the knot first. Pinch the rope with the thumb and two or three fingers of one hand, palm facing toward you. With the other hand, pinch the rope from the other side, palm facing away and the thumb pointing opposite the other (photo 6.11.A). In one smooth motion, rotate your hands together to form two loops (photo 6.11.B). Voila!

When attaching to a D-shaped carabiner, look to see which strand will be loaded and slip that side of the knot on first; this loads the carabiner's spine which is stronger (photo 6.11.C). With a post, ring, or round-end carabiner, it doesn't matter. Pull both strands firmly to set securely.

Technique #2

Crossed Hands: Equally easy. Grasp the rope with your left hand. Cross your right hand over and grab the rope (photo 6.12.A). (Thumbs are pointing away from each other.) Without letting go of the rope, uncross your hands and bring your knuckles together (photo 6.12.B).

Technique #3

One-Handed: A one-handed method for hitching a carabiner is handy at times but takes practice. The actual procedure depends upon which hand you use and the direction the gate is facing. Here is one method: Clip the rope into an anchored carabiner with the gate facing right. Pinch the rear strand with your right hand, palm facing away and thumb pointed downwards (photo 6.13.A). Rotate your wrist up and around until the palm is facing the gate (photo 6.13.B). Steady the carabiner with your fingers and push the loop on with your thumb.

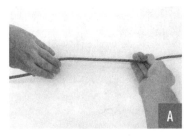
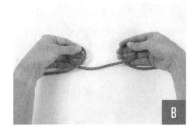

6.11 Clove Hitch, Technique #1, Finger Twirl

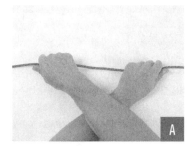
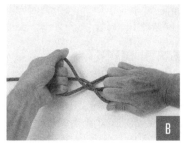

6.12 Clove Hitch, Technique #2, Crossed Hands

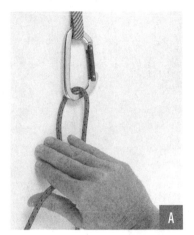

6.13 Clove Hitch, Technique #3, One-Handed

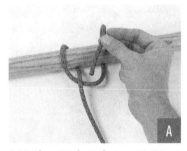

6.14 Clove Hitch, Technique #4, Direct

Technique #4

Direct: Sometimes you will want to tie straight to the anchor point. Pass the end of the rope around the object and cross the strands (photo 6.14.A). Continuing in the same direction of rotation, make another pass around the object but go diagonally across the rope. Slip the end through the new loop (photo 6.14.B).

GIRTH HITCH

Annoyingly, this simple knot goes by other names that have little meaning. It is a handy knot for connecting loops of rope or webbing or attaching loops to anchors. However, the girth hitch is exceedingly dangerous if only one strand is weighted because it slips at very low loads.

Other Names
Lark's head
Cow hitch
Ring hitch

Advantages
Fast way to join two runners. Ideal for attaching a runner to a climbing harness, the haul loop of a pack, or a tree.

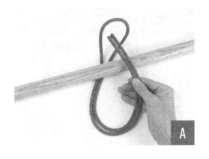

Disadvantages
Can be insecure when only one strand is loaded. The girth hitch should never be used when rigging a belay with the climbing rope.

When used to connect runners, the sharp bends of the girth hitch reduce strength of rope or webbing considerably. Girth hitched runners are 30 percent weaker than runners connected by a carabiner. Girth hitching a runner onto a steel cable, such as a wired stopper, is a recipe for disaster. If you must extend a wire and are short on carabiners, it is better to double the runner through the cable (and not fall).

6.15 Girth Hitch

Technique
Pass the runner around the object. Poke the rest of the runner through the bight that emerges on the other side (photo 6.15.A). Rotate the hitch around the anchor point until the strands are not bent by the bight (photo 6.15.B). Tighten.

If connecting two runners, girth hitch one around the other. Flip the bight forward to make a square knot, then dress and set (photo 6.15.C).

BOWLINE LOOP

The bowline is among the most useful of all knots, with too many iterations to count (a few appear here and in the next chapter). Whether you are a hiker, climber, or boater, the basic single bowline (*boh-lin*) is an important knot to know. The bowline will not slip at high loads unless the rope is especially slippery or stiff. And it is easy to untie afterward.

The single bowline is my favorite for tying into a climbing rope, in part because I've used it for over three decades. Unlike other knots, I can tie it when exhausted, at night, with frozen fingers, and with shaking, mitten-covered hands—all important considerations for hikers and boaters too. Even after extreme and prolonged stress, such as repeated falls, the knot unties easily. For two decades, the single bowline was used in the UIAA drop test to hold an 80-kilogram weight, and such test falls are far harder than anything you'll ever take.

There are at least a half dozen techniques for tying a single bowline, which may contribute to why so many people have a hard time remembering one. Perhaps the most confusing is the bunny/hole/tree thing; I watch people struggle with that method all the time.

To be accurate, the knot under discussion should be called the "inside bowline" (or "right-hand bowline"). The distinction is that the tail always lies inside the loop. If the tail is outside the loop, the knot tends to be less secure (more prone to snagging), though it can be just as strong or even stronger. Indeed, the "outside bowline" (a.k.a. the "Dutch marine," "cowboy," or "left-hand" bowline) may work better for shock cord.

Advantages

The bowline is an excellent tie-in knot for climbers when properly tied, which means *always* snugged and backed up. It is also a good loop knot for anchoring to a tree (add a round turn), attaching a line to a tarp, or just about anything else that requires a temporary loop.

The bowline is convenient for tying off to large objects such as boulders, because you form the knot after the rope is passed around the object. (With a figure-eight loop, part of the knot must be tied first and then repositioned.)

With a little practice, you can tie a bowline with one hand; a valuable skill that could save your life if you scramble into an awkward spot and someone tosses you a line.

Disadvantages

Must have a backup knot when a life is at stake. Many climbers have died or been seriously injured because they failed to tie the bowline properly. If it isn't tight and the backup knot is missing or insecure, the bowline is very dangerous.

The knot can accidentally be tied as an outside bowline, which may be less secure, particularly in laid rope. Fortunately it is easily corrected by pulling the bunny out of the hole and going the other way around the tree.

Avoid loading only the loop (for example, clipping two carabiners in and pulling them apart) because the knot can capsize if forces are high.

Technique #1

Hand Flick: When the knot is tied with the loop toward you, things are super easy. Pass the rope around your waist or through your harness with the end on the right side (reverse everything if you are a lefty). Hold the end in your right hand with the rope parallel to your fingers (photo 6.16.A). Cross your hand over the rope, with the end on top and your thumb below (photo 6.16.B). Now flick your wrist downward until your palm is facing up (photo 6.16.C). The hole now has the end already inside and pointed in the right direction, so just pass the end beneath the rope and back through the hole (photo 6.16.D). Adjust the loop to size and tension the knot (photo 6.16.E). Inspect the knot and if it's an outside bowline (photo 6.16.F), just reverse the direction of the end around the rope.

For tying in, the tail should be about 12 to 18 inches (30 to 45 cm) long. Use this to tie a single or double overhand around the nearest strand of the loop. Butt this backup knot against the bowline and snug it all up (photo 6.16.G). (Many texts show the backup away from the bowline, but that just allows loosening.)

Technique #2

Slipping the Bow: Tying the bowline from the opposite direction (loop away from you) is remarkably complex—everything looks bassackwards—until you learn the trick. Pass the end around the object and then tie a loose slip knot on the rope side, with the sliding part going to the rope (photo 6.17.A). Stick the end of the rope through the noose of the slip knot and grab it again (photo 6.17.B). Give a quick tug on the rope and the slip knot collapses into a bowline (sometimes it snags and needs a helping hand) (photo 6.17.C).

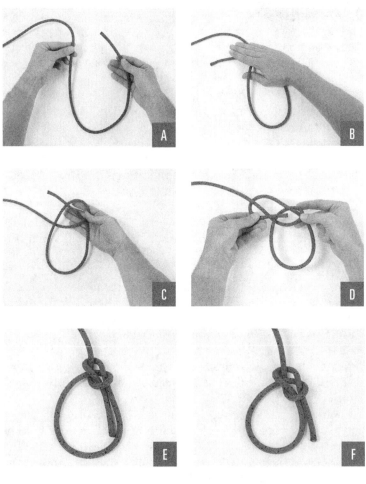

Variations

Double Bowline: Although a properly tied single bowline is sufficient, some climbers prefer the slight extra security of the double bowline. Also called a round turn bowline, the additional loop grips the rope tighter, which is particularly useful with slippery polypro ropes.

6.16 Bowline Loop, Technique #1, Hand Flick

Without holding the end, use the hand-flick technique to form the first loop. Then pull a second loop up to match the first (photo 6.18.A). Thread the end as usual (photo 6.18.B), and tie a backup knot.

Yosemite Bowline: This is another way of backing up either a single or double bowline, but it should not be used with stiff ropes. Tie your bowline as normal but pass the end under to the outside of the loop, cross it over to the inside, and trace the path of the rope out so the strands are parallel (photo 6.19.A). Snug everything up tight (photo 6.19.B).

WATER KNOT

This is the recommended bend for joining the ends of webbing either to make a runner or to extend the length. Because of the knot's propensity for loosening with jostling, it is important to leave the tails several inches long and set the knot very tight.

Avoid the water knot for join-

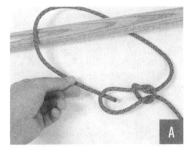

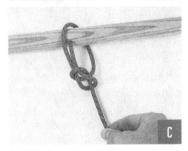

6.17 Bowline Loop, Technique #2, Slipping the Bow

6.18 Double Bowline

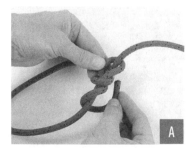

6.19 Yosemite Bowline

ing two ropes if high strength security is required. The rope's round shape allows the knot to be tied in two different forms; they look similar, but one is decidedly inferior. Use a double fisherman's or other good bends in such situations.

Other Names
Ring Bend
Tape Knot

Advantages
A low-bulk knot for webbing that is easy to tie and strong. Equally important, the water knot can be untied when you need to thread an end of webbing through a hole or run a sling around a rock or other object too big to girth hitch. (A double fisherman's in webbing is almost impossible to loosen.)

Disadvantages
The water knot seems to untie itself when you aren't looking (strange things happen inside packs). The knot needs to be set very firmly and rechecked often. Even when properly tied and tightened, most webbing made with HMPE is too slippery to hold standard knots.

Technique
Loosely tie an overhand knot in one end of the webbing, ensuring no twists. Adjust the tail to about 3 inches (8 cm) long (photo 6.20.A). Run your hand down the entire length to remove any twists. Feed the other end through the knot (photo 6.20.B) and follow its path (photo 6.20.C). Carefully tighten all four strands emerging from the knot (use your full body weight if possible) and make certain tails are no less than 2 inches long (photo 6.20.D).

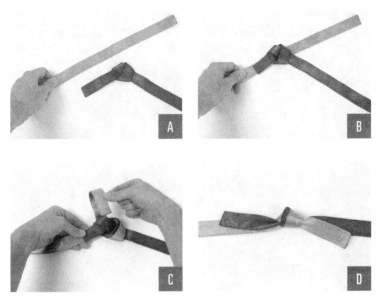

6.20 Water Knot

Some climbers tape the tails (with the ends exposed for a visual check) to the webbing to prevent creep. Do not stitch the ends down since that eliminates a key advantage. With 1-inch tubular webbing, the knot can be tied by pushing an end inside the other (called a "beer knot"); there are no tails flapping, but it is difficult to check.

TAUTLINE HITCH
Everybody needs a good sliding knot. Whether setting up a tent, tying gear onto a truck, or tensioning a handline, an adjustable loop gets the job done. The tautline is essentially a clove hitch with a couple of extra wraps on one side. It is easy to tie and works well most of the time. There are many permutations to the tautline hitch—if one doesn't work with a particular rope, try another.

Advantages
Simple yet effective with smaller diameter cord. More turns can be added if greater friction is required.

Disadvantages
Works poorly with stiff ropes. Doesn't grip as well as line tensioners on icy guylines.

Technique

Pass the rope around the anchor. Wrap the end two or three times around the rope, spiraling into the loop (photo 6.21.A). Bring the end to the other side of the knot and make a half hitch (photo 6.21.B). Snug all the spirals (photo 6.21.C). The knot should slide easily up and down the line when moved by hand yet grip when the loop is tensioned.

Variations

Adjustable Grip Hitch: Similar in function to the tautline, this version can grip better on some ropes. Start as with the tautline, but instead of making a half hitch above the knot, pass the end around the other strand of the loop and tie the half hitch around that (photo 6.22).

Guyline Hitch: So simple it is hard to believe it works so well with slippery line. Tie an overhand knot in the line, then another a couple inches away (photo 6.23.A). Pass the end around the anchor point and then feed it into the outer knot, heading back toward the anchor. Go straight through the second knot (photo 6.23.B). Tighten the loop by pulling on the end.

PRUSIK HITCH

Although the Prusik was once the hitch of choice for ascending ropes, there are better alterna-

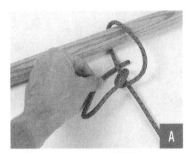

6.21 Tautline Hitch

6.22 Adjustable Grip Hitch

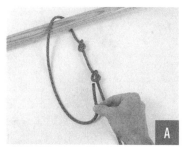 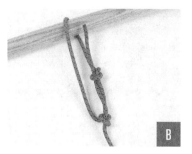

6.23 Guyline Hitch

tives. However, the Prusik is still useful for times when you want a variable position loop in the middle of a line. The Prusik is also widely used for rigging ropes to raise victims in rescues; if something goes wrong, the knot will slip rather than break or cut the rope as can happen with mechanical ascenders. This knot was developed by Dr. Karl Prusik around 1918, but as with many simple knots that have modern names, it is likely much, much older.

Advantages
Very fast to tie and easy to remember. Omnidirectional, so the pull can come from almost any angle.

Disadvantages
Less effective than other grip knots when the pull comes from only one direction. Not a good choice for loops made of webbing. If a small diameter cord is used, the Prusik can set so tight it is very difficult to release.

Technique
For use on 10- to 11-mm climbing and caving ropes, Prusik loops are normally made from 6-mm accessory cord that is tied with a double fisherman's to make loops 12 to 18 inches (30 to 45 cm) long. Smaller diameter cord works but tends to set too tight while larger cord may need extra turns. Webbing works better with other friction hitches, such as the Hedden or klemheist (Chapter 7).

Girth hitch the sling around the rope but do not tighten (photo 6.24.A). Open the girth by spreading it apart and make one or two more wraps around the rope. Snug it all up, making sure none of the wraps cross (photo 6.24.B), and carefully apply weight to confirm that the Prusik holds.

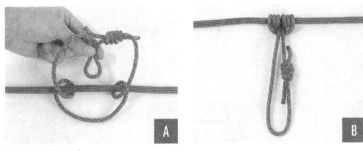

6.24 Prusik Hitch

TIMBER HITCH

Useful for hauling logs (hence its name), this simple hitch can also serve as a quick, temporary attachment to many anchor points. It can hold a substantial load yet remain easy to loosen.

Advantages

The harder you pull, the tighter it grabs.

Disadvantages

•The knot is totally dependent upon friction, so a slick rope or smooth anchor point may be less secure.

Technique

Pass the rope end around the object and tie a loose half hitch. Spiral the rope end three or four more times around the loop (photo 6.25.A). When you pull, the spirals will spread out and pinch against the object (photo 6.25.B). To give more directional control when pulling a log or big rock, toss a half hitch over the end of the object and position it about a foot away from the first knot (photo 6.25.C).

SQUARE LASHING

The fine art of lashing poles together has allowed humans to engineer everything from forts and ballistae to bridges and towers. Even today, bamboo is lashed to create massive scaffoldings used for construction in much of Asia. The outdoorsperson may need to lash together a stretcher for evacuating someone who is injured or build an emergency lean-to for shelter.

The square lashing is used whenever poles intersect at right angles, so it is the most common form. Since horizontal beams may need to bear significant loads, an improvised lashing may let you down . . . with a big crash.

Advantages

Best way to bind a horizontal pole to a vertical pole.

Disadvantages

Can strangle a live tree if left in place; use natural fiber rope if it must be left in place. For building a tree house, use lag bolts instead of lashings or nails.

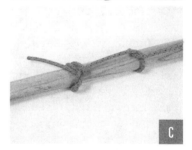

Technique

Tie a clove hitch (or a timber hitch) around the vertical post (photo 6.26.A). Lay the crossbeam above the knot and bring the rope over the beam, behind the post, down over the beam on the other side, and then behind the post below the clove hitch (photo 6.26.B). Repeat this lashing turn three times, pulling the rope tight each time (photo 6.26.C). Now make three

6.25 Timber Hitch

frapping turns around the lashing and crank the knot tighter each time (photo 6.26.D). Finish off with another clove hitch around the crossbeam; make one half hitch, snug it, then make one more and snug (photo 6.26.E).

DIAGONAL LASHING

With only right angles, a structure will fold and collapse, so you must add cross braces for integrity.

Advantages

Most secure method of adding diagonal braces to a structure.

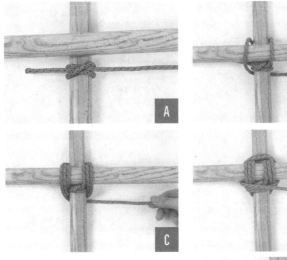

Technique

Cross the two poles and tie a simple hitch horizontally around both (photo 6.27.A). Continue wrapping for three turns (photo 6.27.B), then wrap vertically for three turns (photo 6.27.C). Now make three frapping turns around the lashing and finish with a clove hitch (photo 6.27.D).

6.26 Square Lashing

SHEAR LASHING

Say you break a tent pole and don't have any duct tape (gasp!)—a shear lashing can save the night. This is also a good way to build an antennae mast for a base camp when the available wood is too short. And the shear lashing is the best way to build an A-frame or a tripod structure from raft oars.

Advantages

Ideal for splinting broken poles, extending a pole, or creating an A-frame.

Technique

Lay two poles next to each other, propped up off the ground for access, and make a clove hitch around one. Start wrapping around the

6.27 Diagonal Lashing

poles for six to ten turns until the lashing is as wide as the two poles (photo 6.28.A). If you are splinting or extending a pole, pull the lashing snug after each wrap; for an A-frame, leave them a bit loose. Make two frapping turns between the poles around all the lashings and finish with two half hitches (photo 6.28.B). For the A-frame, splay the poles apart to the desired position and then tighten the frapping turns; a cross brace may be needed to hold them apart. If a pole is being extended, the two should overlap considerably with a second shear lashing added.

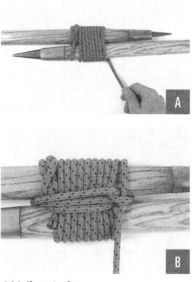

6.28 Shear Lashing

Variation

Tripod Lashing: This is essentially the same as shear lashing except with three poles instead of two. However, when you raise the structure, there are three possible ways for the poles to cross. The strongest is formed when the two end poles cross below the center pole, which lies in the resulting notch. This gives a wood-on-wood contact that bears some load while the other possibilities put all of the strain on the lashings.

Knots for Climbing

Whether you enjoy scrambling to a remote summit or dangling from a vertical face, it is good to have a core knowledge of climbing knots. As you spend more time in the rock and alpine world, having a larger repertoire of knots is necessary for efficiency and safety. And a few knots are handy to know even if you use them only once in a blue moon.

ANCHORS

A complete discussion on building anchors for climbing and caving is beyond the scope of this book. However, it behooves scramblers, paddlers, and others with an occasional need to have a basic understanding of anchor systems.

Unless you are tying off a rope to a healthy tree larger in diameter than your thigh or a boulder the size of a VW, it is smart to share the load among multiple anchor points. It is equally smart to make certain the entire anchor will not fail if one point pulls loose.

There are two basic rigging methods for building a multipoint anchor: the sliding-X and the cordelette.

When evaluating an anchor, it is important to look at the entire system and not just at the individual components. To assist frazzled brains, pick one of two mnemonics (either one works): EARNEST (Equal tension, Angles appropriate, Redundant, Non-Extending, Strong, Timely); or SRENE (Strong, Redundant, Equalized, Non-Extending). The idea is that, should one anchor point fail, the others will do the job; backups are provided and shock loading is minimized. Every anchor is unique and does not necessarily have to meet all the recommendations—but each must be considered before ruling a component unnecessary.

Single-Point Anchor

A sturdy tree, solid post, or immovable rock may be all the anchor you need, depending upon the application and potential forces. When rigging a rappel or a top-rope anchor, a girth-hitched runner (see Girth Hitch, Chapter 6) will suffice since the loads, even in a worst-case scenario, are moderate.

A better option, given sufficient sling length, is to double the runner around the anchor point and clip both bights with a locking carabiner. If the angle between the bights is less than 90 degrees, this offers significantly more strength than the girth hitch. However, wider angles from too short a runner place the carabiner at great risk of crossloading on a weak axis, reducing the entire chain to its weakest link. To make the system more secure, hold the bights together and tie an overhand or figure eight to create a master clip point.

If extremely high loads are possible, as in rescue situations or rigging a tyrolean traverse, then take the time to rig a three-wrap/pulltwo anchor. Untie the knot in a long runner, then use the webbing or cord to make three entire wraps around a stout tree. Tie the ends together with a water or double fisherman's bend and pull out the other two strands (pull the knot against the front of the tree).

Sliding-X Anchor

If there are two solid anchor points, such as a pair of bolts or stoppers in perfect crack placements, you can quickly create a single, equalizing master anchor point. This requires a runner (loop of webbing or accessory cord) and three or four carabiners. However, the sliding-X is neither redundant (it's all over if the sling breaks) nor nonextending (if one anchor pops, the other is in for a serious jolt), so it should not be used when high forces are possible and anchors are suspect.

Clip one carabiner into each anchor, then clip the runner into each carabiner. Put a finger over the top strand between the two anchors and slide down until you are pulling on both strands of the loop at the center. Now the critical step: Hook a finger over only one strand and make a 180-degree twist. Finish by clipping the third carabiner through both the twisted and untwisted strands (photo 7.1.A). Alternatively, you can clip the third carabiner into one strand, then rotate the carabiner to face the other direction and clip it to the other strand. This is faster but a little harder to check visually.

If you merely clip the carabiner over the two strands and one of the anchor points fails, the carabiner will slide right off the end . . . and somebody may die. With a twist in one loop forming an X, an anchor point failure keeps the carabiner inside the loop, making survival possible if the remaining anchor holds. This setup allows the master anchor to slide around as the direction of loading changes, keeping the forces evenly distributed (photo 7.1.B).

Always use at least one locking carabiner at the master anchor point (sometimes called the power point). If a locker is unavailable, use two carabiners with the gates opposite and opposed.

The sliding-X also works with three anchor points if the runner is long enough. Just clip the runner into all three carabiners and run a finger along either side of the center anchor to divide the runner into thirds. Make a twist in each of the two cen-

7.1 Sliding-X Anchor

tral bights to make loops. Clip the two loops and the remaining strand with the primary carabiner(s).

With either a two- or three-anchor sliding-X, it is important that the runner is long enough. The angle between the outer bights should be 90 degrees or less to reduce the load on each anchor point. When the angle is 120 degrees, each anchor point receives 100 percent of the forces, and wider angles multiply the forces tremendously.

Above all, never just clip the runner into two anchor points and clip a third carabiner into the loop, leaving a straight strand between the anchor points. This is called the American Death Triangle and it places dangerously high forces upon the anchor. If you find a rappel anchor rigged in this manner, destroy it and rig properly.

Cordelette Anchor

Although the sliding-X divides the load equally among anchors even when the direction changes, the drawback is that failure of one anchor point places a sudden, violent load upon the remaining anchor(s). One popular solution is to use a longer runner called a cordelette.

Clip the cordelette into all three anchor points, place a finger on either side of the center carabiner, and pull until there are three equal bights (photo 7.2.A). Pull with your fingers to equalize the loops in the direction of loading, grab all the loops in the other hand, and tie them all together with an overhand loop to create a power point (photo 7.2.B).

A cordelette anchor spreads the load evenly among three anchor points. Even if one fails, the other two still function normally without the sling extending, so the shock load is greatly reduced. The drawback is the sling is no longer self-equalizing, so you must anticipate the direction of loading before tying the central knot. If the force comes

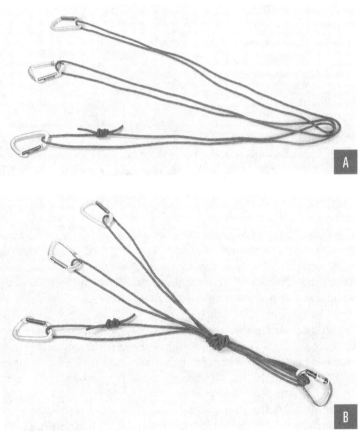

7.2 Cordelette Anchor

from a different direction, a single anchor point may take most of the load; be extra cautious if the anchors are nuts or cams.

There is no advantage of tying a figure-eight loop instead of an overhand unless the sling is very long and you need to shorten it. Testing of cordelette anchors with one failure point shows the overhand does the job just fine. When the anchor points are too far apart to tie a standard cordelette, a bowline-on-a-bight can be employed.

A cordelette is typically tied with a double or triple fisherman's bend (depending upon the core material). The cord is usually about 21 feet (6.4 meters) of either 7-mm nylon (only costs about $8) or one of the high tech 5- to 6-mm cords, which are about half the weight and bulk but cost about $22 to $35. Using thicker nylon, versus the high-strength cord, gives the anchor system roughly the same strength and more capability to absorb shock; particularly important in rescue operations.

A "webolette" is a compact alternative that is made of 10 to 12 feet of nylon or HMPE webbing with a loop sewn into each end. Never make a pseudo-cordelette from a single strand of accessory cord with loops tied on the ends. Sewn webbing is full-strength, but with tied cord the entire belay anchor is reduced to the strength of a single knotted strand—less than half that of a full loop and well within reach of conceivable forces. Not good.

RAPPEL KNOTS

Whether climbing, caving, or canyoneering, there is often a need for connecting two ropes to allow longer rappels. Sometimes ropes are also joined to allow top roping (slingshot belay) on tall cliffs. In all of these situations, failure of the knot will probably kill someone.

At first glance, the logical conclusion might be to use the strongest knot possible; the double fisherman's is the traditional favorite. However, there are three other factors to consider: The knot must be easy to tie, it must stay tied yet remain easy to untie, and it must not get stuck easily.

For standard rappelling situations, the greatest load likely to be applied to the knot is about 440 pounds (200 kilograms). This would be the case with two climbers simulrapping (each rappelling on a single strand counterbalancing the other) or perhaps a single climber with a massive haul bag, making small hops on the descent. Even when top roping, it is doubtful higher forces can be achieved without climbing above the anchor. Thus massive knot strength is not needed.

What is essential is a knot that will stay tied under any circumstances, preferably without the need for backups. When the situation dictates that a stuck rope is unlikely, rope drag is not a factor in retrieval, and time is not critical, then a stout knot like the double fisherman's or figure-nine bend makes sense. When you don't have those luxuries (more often than not), the offset overhand bend has the advantage.

If you aren't sure the rope ends reach the ground, be certain to add a stopper knot at the end of each strand. When things are particularly dicey (rappeling at night, in a storm, or in areas with rockfall), a rappel backup knot attached between rope and harness is highly recommended. This will lock in case you are knocked unconscious and jam if you happen to reach the stopper knots.

To use a rappel backup, the best method is to extend the rappel device with a runner so that it's about chest level (and no higher than your head). Then tie a friction hitch below the rappel device and clip it with a carabiner to a leg loop. This is *not* something that can be easily improvised: the system must be figured out ahead of time and tested. If the friction hitch's sling is too long, it can be sucked into the rappel device; too short and it will be in the wrong place for controlling descent speed with the brake hand.

The advantage of attaching the friction hitch below the rappel device is that friction in the device does most of the work so the hitch is easy to release once employed. A Prusik above the device (old-school method) can lock up and leave you stranded in midair, requiring some tricks to get going, and there is a tendency to panic and grab the knot in front of you, causing it to release. The only drawback to the below-device method is care must be exercised passing overhangs; if the extended device gets trapped above the lip, freeing it will be a real hassle.

TIE-IN KNOTS

Your tie-in knot is your life. It's that simple. Screw it up and you crater. Over the years, many climbers have died or been hurt from improperly tied knots. Others have been seriously injured after starting their knot, getting distracted, and failing to finish it before climbing. Whichever knot you use to tie in, *stop talking* and focus! Get in the habit of checking your partners' knots before they set out.

Even though the forces can be many times greater than when rappelling, strength is not a real issue for an appropriate tie-in knot. Getting it right 100 percent of the time and having it stay tied are what count; ease of untying afterward is a desirable bonus. When I tie in, I usually use a single bowline because I know I can get it right without thinking; the motion is programmed in my brain. Personally, I have a harder time with the figure-eight loop when I'm tired, on edge, or can't see what I'm doing.

There are numerous knots that can be used to tie-in safely. While you may decide that the framfroogle is the perfect choice, oddball knots make it difficult for your belayer to give a quick visual check before you set off. Both the figure eight and bowline are well known and easy to visually check, so they are the standards.

Always thread the rope through both the leg loops and waist belt of your harness. This part of the harness receives the most wear so it is heavily reinforced. Although the belay loop is plenty strong (do not buy a harness without one), it should not be used to tie in.

For tying into the middle of the rope—standard practice for glacier travel—it is best to tie a butterfly loop and clip two locking carabiners (or a single dual-action autolock) into it and the belay loop. Attaching a carabiner to leg loops and waist belt makes outward loading of the gate, and complete failure, possible. Some climbers just use a bight of the rope and tie directly in with a bowline.

Clipping into the end of the rope is common when top roping at gyms and crags, particularly with lots of students swapping ropes. Several people are now paraplegics because their screw-gate or single-action autolock managed to open when they fell. While it is preferable to teach proper knots, if a climber must clip in, use a dual action locking carabiner (requires a twist and pull) and a figure-eight loop.

CLIMBER'S FIGURE-EIGHT LOOP

The figure-eight loop is certainly the most popular knot these days for tying a climbing rope to a harness. It is easy to teach and will stay tied without requiring a backup knot.

Other Names
Figure-eight follow-through
Rewoven, retraced, or rethreaded figure eight
Flemish loop

Advantages
Nearly idiotproof.

Disadvantages
After several small falls or a single hard one (high fall factor), the normal figure eight can be extremely difficult to untie. The version described here prevents some of those struggles.

Forgetting to untie the knot before pulling the rope down usually results in a stuck rope and much embarrassment. Several climbers have proven the hard way that it's still possible to mess up a figure eight. Failing to finish the knot means hitting the deck.

Technique

Hold the tip of the rope in your fingers and extend your arm to the side. Grab the rope with the other hand at about the position of your heart and tie a figure eight. Thread the end of the rope through the harness and pull it till the knot is about to jam against the harness loops. Lead the end back through the knot to make the loop (photo 7.3.A), following all the turns so the tail is parallel to the rope (photo 7.3.B). Take a moment to dress the knot.

A backup knot is not necessary if the figure eight has several inches of tail and you cinch it down by pulling firmly on *both* strand pairs: This knot is not coming untied. Adding a double overhand as some texts recommend just puts a hard knot out front to whack you.

If you still want a backup, a better alternative is to use an extra pass. After you have tied the figure eight, bring the tail so that it follows the upper portion of the knot around the standing rope (photo 7.3.C) and then tuck it back into the knot next to the strands coming

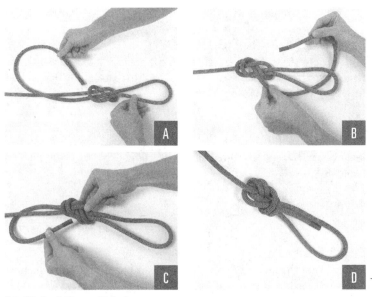

7.3 Climber's Figure-Eight Loop

from your harness (photo 7.3.D). This secures the tail, makes the knot easier to untie, and only takes a few extra seconds.

BUTTERFLY LOOP

An under-appreciated knot, the butterfly is a jack-of-all-trades. Unlike most other loop knots, the butterfly does not deform when the two rope strands are pulled apart. The farmer's loop and harness loop are related but not quite the same; nice but less symmetrical.

Other Names

Alpine butterfly
Lineman's loop
Wireman's knot

Advantages

Omnidirectional and secure. Two simple ways to tie it. (There is a third method, but it requires an end so there is no real advantage.)

Disadvantages

Sometimes difficult to untie after heavy loading.

Technique #1

Rope Twist: Make a bight in the rope and then twist with two rotations of your wrist (photo 7.4.A). Fold the bight over to the front and pass the end of the bight underneath the lower crossing (photo 7.4.B). Bring the bight to the rear and poke it through the gap between the two crossings (photo 7.4.C). Pull the bight up and dress (photo 7.4.D).

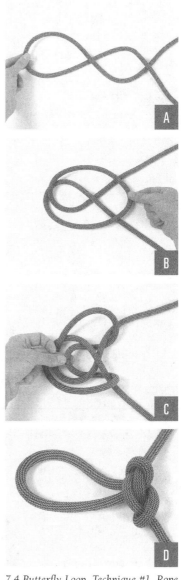

7.4 Butterfly Loop, Technique #1, Rope Twist

Technique #2

Hand Wrap: Though I had observed this method for ages, it was hard to remember until I realized the sequence could be summed up: outside in, outside over, and through.

Drape the rope across your hand. Make two wraps of the rope around your hand (photo 7.5.A). Pick up either outside coil and set it in between the other two (photo 7.5.B). Now take the new outside loop (was center), pass it over the other two (photo 7.5.C) (photo 7.5.D), and then tuck it through the wraps. Remove your hand and snug it all up.

Variation

Double Butterfly Loop: As with many loop knots, both two- and three-loop versions of the butterfly are possible. Using the hand-wrap technique, add one more wrap around your hand. Now tie the knot treating the middle two loops as one.

This results in two anchor loops (photo 7.6) that are very easy to adjust and equalize, unlike a double figure eight or a bowline-on-a-bight. To increase the length of either loop, simply feed more rope in from one direc-

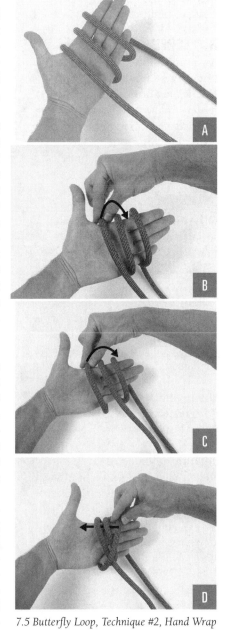

7.5 Butterfly Loop, Technique #2, Hand Wrap

tion. Before untying, equalize the loops to minimize confusion. This is a convenient knot for setting up quick belay stations.

MUNTER HITCH

An absolutely essential knot for any climber, the Munter hitch is also useful for hikers and boaters. The fric-tion created by the knot

7.6 Double Butterfly Loop

allows a falling climber to be safely caught or a heavy mass easily lowered.

When the Munter is "closed"—that is both strands of the rope are next to each other (photo 7.7.A)—it has a braking force of about 2.5 kN, which is greater than many belay devices (around 2.0 kN). An "open Munter," however, in which the strands are on opposite sides of the hitch (photo 7.7.B), has a braking force of about 1.4 kN. This means the belay is a bit more dynamic yet it still offers much more braking force than a waist belay (about 0.8 kN).

The hitch is mistakenly named after Werner Munter, a Swiss guide who helped popularize it in the United States. But this knot has been around for thousands of years and a German climber, Franz Ruso, is said to have discovered its usefulness for belaying. It was called the "Seilkreuzbremse" (rope cross belay) in a 1966 German military climbing manual and was introduced in 1974 to the UIAA at a meeting in Italy (hence one of its names). Few European climbers know it as the Munter hitch unless they've spent a lot of time with Americans.

7.7 Munter Hitch

Other Names
Italian, dynamic, friction, or backhanded hitch
Demi-capstan
HMS knot
Halbmastwurfsicherung (HMS, German)
Mezzo barcaiolo (Italian), *demi-cabestan* (French)

Advantages
Needs only one locking carabiner to deliver an effective belay. Numerous applications for rescue and lowering heavy loads.

Disadvantages
Requires a pear-shaped HMS locking carabiner except in cases of dire emergency. Standard lockers do not have a large, round end, so the knot will not rotate easily.

Twists ropes badly when used to rappel with the brake hand off to the side. (Running the rope between your legs prevents this. Extend the carabiner to chest height with a runner to give your brake hand room.)

Technique #1
Clove Twirl: Clip the HMS carabiner to the belay loop of your harness. Tie a clove hitch using the finger twirl (photo 7.8.A) (see Technique #1 for Clove Hitch, Chapter 6). Orient the knot so that the loop leading to the climber will be clipped first. Back the other loop off a half turn and clip both strands into the carabiner (photo 7.8.B).

Technique #2
One-handed: Clip the rope into an anchored HMS carabiner at the belay station. Grab the rope with your brake hand by rotating the wrist outward (clockwise for the right hand, counter for the left), thumb pointed down (photo 7.9.A). Roll your wrist over (photo 7.9.B), snagg

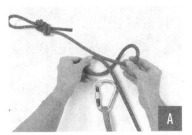
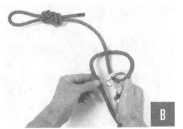

7.8 Munter Hitch, Technique #1, Clove Twirl

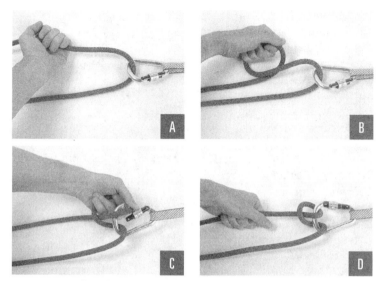

7.9 Munter Hitch, Technique #2, One-Handed

the carabiner with your fingers and push the loop into the gate in one smooth motion (photo 7.9.C) (photo 7.9.D).

DOUBLE FISHERMAN'S BEND

A longtime favorite for semipermanently joining two ropes. The double fisherman's is ideal for tying the slings on stoppers and hexes since the knot does not need to be re-checked. Once this bend sets, the ropes are practically welded together.

Other Names
Grapevine knot

Advantages
Oh, so secure. The best knot for slinging chocks and making Prusik loops. Once tied and set, you can pretty much forget about it accidentally coming undone.

Disadvantages
Oh, such a pain to untie. Many people struggle to get the second half of this knot properly oriented. Not recommended for rappel or top-rope setups unless you enjoy a good struggle. Makes a bulky, ungainly, albeit permanent, knot when used for webbing.

Technique

Tie a double overhand (just add a wrap before completing an overhand knot) about a foot from the end of one rope and pull it snug but not tight (photo 7.10.A). Poke the end of the other rope through the hole (some eliminate this step by tying the first knot around the other rope; it's a tossup). Tie another double overhand around the first rope in the opposite direction (follow the direction of the first knot's inner loop) (photo 7.10.B) (photo 7.10.C). When the ropes are pulled, the two knots will snuggle nicely together.

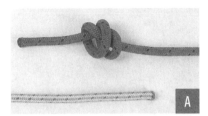

Adjust the tails of both knots: Make them about 2 inches (5 cm) long for accessory cord, longer for bigger ropes. One at a time, pull each of the four strands tight until the knot is a dense, compact barrel (photo 7.10.D).

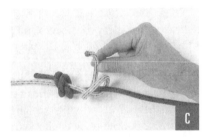

Variation

Triple Fisherman's: When making slings from cord that has an HMPE or aramid core, an extra wrap is required for each knot.

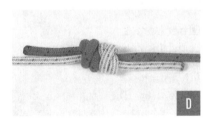

7.10 Double Fisherman's Bend

FIGURE-NINE BEND

When used to join two kernmantle ropes, the figure-nine bend is easier to untie than either a Flemish (figure-eight) bend or double fisherman's. The intertwining of the ropes inspires confidence without the bulk of a square fisherman's.

Advantages

Secure yet relatively easy to untie. Slightly less jam-prone than a double fisherman's or square fisherman's bend.

Disadvantages

A bit of a puzzle, this knot requires careful attention to tie properly. May not work with some rope material/diameter/construction combinations—test before risking bodily harm!

Technique

Tie a figure-nine in the end of one rope; that is, start forming a figure-eight but make an extra half wrap around the rope (photo 7.11.A). Next thread the other rope from the tail and retrace the first rope's path (photo 7.11.B). Take a moment to make sure all the strands are parallel and uncrossed (photo 7.11.C), then start pulling them one at a time until the knot is drawn up snug (photo 7.11.D). When you untie the first rope's knot, you'll find the second knot is actually a timber hitch.

OFFSET OVERHAND BEND

Stuck rappel ropes are the things epics are made of. Do what you can to avoid this situation without creating a new worst nightmare. A primary advantage of the offset overhand is that it gives the rope a smooth profile during retrieval. When the knot encounters an edge, it rolls up out of the way without getting caught.

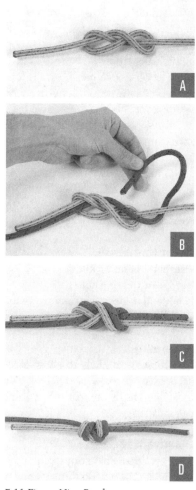

7.11 Figure-Nine Bend

Reading about it in a book is one thing . . . blah, blah, blah, makes sense. Then when you use the offset overhand for the first time and see this huge void below, you quickly understand how this got nicknamed the Euro Death Knot—it's spooky!

But plenty of techweenie climbers with the same fears and tensile machines have tested the heck out of the offset overhand bend. It's been maltreated, soaked in water, and pulled apart with rope combinations of greatly different diameters (such as 7 and 11 mm). I've watched it go up to loads way beyond what is possible in rappels.

And it works. Consistently and reliably . . . as long as it is properly tied. This means long tails. The smaller or more supple rope on the bottom. And the whole thing set tight by sequentially pulling hard on each individual strand.

The offset overhand bend is for expeditious retreats. If you'll do a lot of bouncing around or other shenanigans, by all means use a more secure knot, such as the double fisherman's or figure-nine bend.

Danger: Because the offset overhand bend is so freaky in appearance, some have been tempted to tie a figure eight in the same manner because it appears more secure. Looks can be deceiving and in fact this version has killed. When loaded, the offset figure eight can invert itself at pitifully small loads—it literally keeps turning inside out until the rope creeps off the end. Never, ever use an offset figure eight for any life support roll!

Other Names
Overhand bend or knot
European Death Knot (EDK)
Double, flat, or two-strand overhand knot
Thumb bend

Advantages
Easy to tie, least likely to get stuck, adequately strong and secure. May be used with ropes of different diameters—thoroughly test potential combinations before trusting your life to them. Easy to untie after it has been loaded.

Disadvantages
Scares the bejeebers out of any normal person every time they use it (this would be a good thing). Can come untied if not properly dressed and set.

7.12 Offset Overhand Bend

Technique

Thread one end of a rope through the rappel anchor, usually the skinnier of the two. Hold both rope ends up together. Tie an overhand knot with both ends; the tails will emerge together (photo 7.12.A). Dress the knot so that no strands are crossed and the smaller rope is on the bottom (if it isn't, just push the loops around a bit).

Adjust the tails until they are about 12 inches (30 cm) long (photo 7.12.B). Then, one at a time, pull each strand as tight as you can— think about your family and friends during this step.

The last step before attaching your rappel device is to position the knot at least a foot below the anchor. If it is drawn into the slings, then starting the pull is much harder when time for retrieval.

Variations

All sorts of other offset bends have been proposed. But each has added unneeded levels of complexity and magnified the knot's bulk, defeating the entire purpose.

BOWLINE STOPPER KNOT

Rappelling off the end of a rope when still far above the ground could be your final mistake. Likewise lowering a climber from a climb and not paying attention to an unanchored end can have seriously nasty consequences. Whenever you aren't sure the rope is long enough, a bulky stopper knot is prudent.

Some recommend using a simple figure-eight knot or a double overhand knot as a stopper. However, these can be too compact when snugged and may fly right through some rappel devices. The bowline stopper knot is just as fast to tie but is bulkier and easier to untie after it's been tugged tight (sometimes happens when the stopper knot gets stuck in a crack). Though there is no loop, it's actually a bowline if you look closely.

When rappelling, do not simply tie two rope ends together! This

7.13 Bowline Stopper Knot

prevents twists in the ropes from unwinding and you will end up with a kinked mess at the bottom. It's a bad idea to put a loop knot in the rope ends . . . they love to snag and make your life miserable.

Advantages

Fast to tie and easy to remember; it's an overhand knot on steroids. Bulky enough not to get sucked through most rappel devices. Fast to untie, even after violent tugging.

Disadvantages

Like all stopper knots, it's a crack magnet and loves to get stuck. If you can see that the rope ends reach the ground, a stopper knot is not needed. Be sure to untie any stopper knot before pulling down the rope.

Technique

Tie an overhand knot and let the rope curl back toward itself. The tail will naturally want to go back over the rope. Instead, pass it under the rope and thread it through the hole (photo 7.13.A). Then snug it up (photo 7.13.B).

HEDDEN HITCH

A good friction hitch in the memory banks is vital for climbers and cavers—this knowledge can get you out of trouble. Whitewater enthusiasts may need it some day to recover a pinned boat. Although the Prusik hitch is the best known, it can be problematic when the only objective is moving up (the Prusik is still a good utility knot though).

Even if you have mechanical ascenders, there is one thing they can't do: Grip two ropes at the same time. The Hedden and similar friction hitches allow you to backup a rappel device and stop whenever necessary, whether using one rope or two.

This hitch is named for Chet Hedden, who first described it in 1959. A few years later, it picked up the *kreuzklem* moniker in Germany.

Other Names
Kreuzklem (cross-clamp)
Reverse klemheist

Advantages
The best gripping of the standard friction hitches. Just as easy to tie as the klemheist yet requires fewer wraps.

Disadvantages
No substitute for mechanical ascenders if you have a lot of climbing to do; much more tiring and knot passes are a nuisance. Works well in only one direction; use a Prusik for horizontal or diagonal fixed lines.

Technique
Pinch the bottom end of a sling over the rope(s) and wrap upward (photo 7.14.A), one spiral for accessory cord, two for webbing. Make the spirals neat so no twists are in the sling. Slip the long top bight through the small bottom bight (photo 7.14.B). Snug it all up, then carefully weight the loop (photo 7.14.C).

Variations
Klemheist: While just a minor modification in construction—the bottom loop goes through the top loop (photo 7.15)—the difference in performance between the Hedden and klemheist can be significant. In most cases the klemheist requires one or two additional wraps to equal the grip-

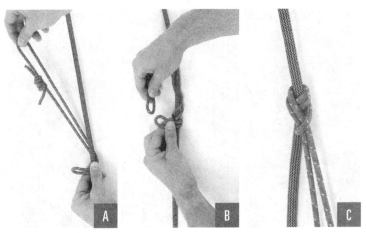

7.14 Hedden Hitch

ping power of the Hedden hitch. Experiment with different combinations of rope, cord, and webbing to see which knot is most effective.

Bachmann Hitch: This is indeed a good friction hitch that has been around for ages, but it has a major caveat. Simply clip the sling into a carabiner, then start wrapping downward around both the rope and the spine of the carabiner (photo 7.16.A). The final wrap emerges from the bottom of the carabiner and that loop is loaded (photo 7.16.B). For more holding power, tie a half hitch around the rope below the carabiner.

7.15 Klemheist

The Bachmann grips well, given sufficient wraps, and it is very easy to slide upward. However, the carabiner is only there for convenience and cannot be used as a handle. Grabbing the carabiner in a moment of panic will send you streaking downward!

Autoblock: Possibly the most overrated knot in the climbing world. This is a sad cross between a Hedden and klemheist, without offering the benefits of either.

The autoblock is recommended in several texts as a good choice for backing up a rappel, but it is very finicky and generally unreliable to work when needed. The autoblock is adequate when used with narrow accessory cord and three to four complete wraps around the rope (photo 7.17); sling length is critical. But webbing is its, and possibly your, downfall. Before pretending this knot will save you in an emergency, test it with your own ropes and gear.

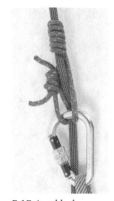

7.16 Bachmann Hitch

7.17 Autoblock

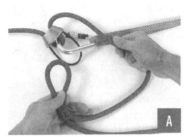

7.18 Mule Knot

MULE KNOT

When belaying climbers, it is sometimes necessary to temporarily secure them so you can use both hands for a task without taking them off belay. If the climber has fallen and is injured, you may have to free yourself to begin a rescue. All of these situations can be handled by a mule knot, which is just a climber's term for a slip knot tie-off of the belay. Tying off the belay is easy when the rope is unweighted, but things are a bit more problematic when a climber is hanging. All climbers should know how to handle this situation.

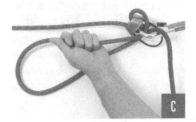

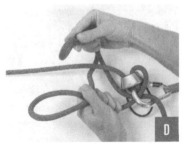

Other Names
Releasable, blocking, or transport knot
Belay tie-off

Advantages
Allows the belayer to free the hands when the climber is not moving. This is the first step in escaping a belay in an emergency.

Disadvantages
When under tension, can pinch fingers if not careful. Two short drops spook whoever is hanging.

Technique

With the loaded rope locked off, move your brake hand up near the belay device. Use your free hand to make a bight in the slack rope and pass this through the belay carabiner (photo 7.18.A). With your free hand, grab the part of the bight nearest the belay hand and move it up near the loaded rope (photo 7.18.B). Quickly remove the belay hand while pulling upward on the loop; there may be a short drop, but the new belay hand has the advantage of two extra bends in the rope as you bring it up parallel to the taut rope (photo 7.18.C).

Pinch a small bight in the slack rope between the index finger and thumb of the belay hand. Reach behind the taut rope and pull some more slack to make another bight. Bring this to the front and push it into the first loop (photo 7.18.D). You now have a slip knot around the loaded rope. Work as much of the slack out as you can, verify that everything is right, and quickly remove your brake hand (photo 7.18.E). Either clip the loop to the main rope with a carabiner or tie an overhand around the rope.

MARINER'S KNOT

When rappelling or lowering, the Mariner's knot is used to transfer the load from one section of rope to another at a knot pass. This technique is also used in rescue situations such as escaping the belay. It was introduced in 1963 by Wastl Mariner in his book, *Mountain Rescue Techniques*.

The Mariner's knot is generally used with a double-length (48-inch) runner of 9/16 to 11/16-inch (14 to 18 mm) nylon webbing, a 36-inch-long Prusik loop made of accessory cord, or a spare cordelette if you have one. Two single-length runners can be girth-hitched together if necessary.

Other Names
Load-releasing hitch

Advantages
An easy method for transferring the weight of a climber from one rope or anchor to another. Can be released when under tension.

Disadvantages
Should not be used with most brands of HMPE webbing; they're too slick. Will untie on its own if tail is not kept under tension or secured.

Technique
The exact procedure depends upon the materials at hand but generally starts with positioning a mechanical ascender or friction hitch, either

with the long runner or another short runner, aimed at the anchor on the tensioned rope. If an HMS carabiner is available at the anchor, use a Munter hitch with the long runner; the preferred option (photo 7.19.A). Otherwise, for standard carabiners, wrap the runner twice

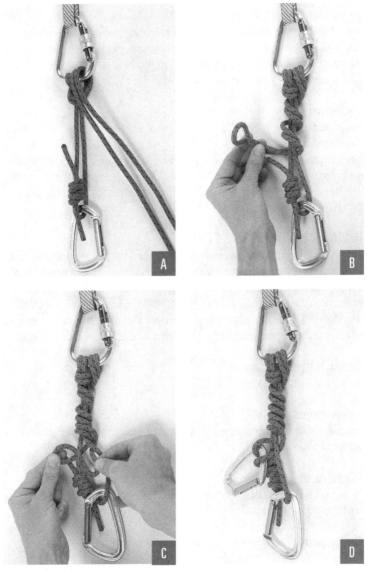

7.19 Mariner's Knot

around the wide end. Wind the tail four to five times around the load-bearing strands of the runner to increase friction (photo 7.19.B).

To secure the Mariner, spread the load-bearing strands apart and push half of the tail through (photo 7.19.C). This creates two small loops in the tail on either side of one load-bearing strand. Clip the two loops with a carabiner (photo 7.19.D).

Now slowly release the tension from the rope and onto the ascender/knot, checking to make sure it grabs. To release the Mariner, unclip the carabiner and then slowly unwind the tail, holding it firmly as the load transfers onto the rope.

Variation
Radium Release Hitch: This performs a similar function of transferring tension in a system but requires a single strand of cord with a figure-eight loop in the end (instead of a big loop). Clip the figure-eight into a carabiner attached to a friction hitch on the rope. Bring the strand through the anchor carabiner, back through the first biner, and up to the anchor. Tie a Munter hitch to the anchor carabiner.

INLINE FIGURE-EIGHT LOOP
When you need a loop that can be pulled parallel to the rope, this knot works well. A normal figure eight works best when both rope strands are pulled together, opposite of the loop. A butterfly knot is at its best when the rope strands are pulled apart and the loop is pulled in a third direction. The inline figure-eight loop gives you the third option; strands pulled apart but the loop loaded in the same direction as one.

Other Names
Directional figure eight

Advantages
Provides a quick, semipermanent loop in a rope when a Prusik sling isn't available.

Disadvantages
If the loop is loaded in the opposite direction, the knot can capsize and become a slip knot.

Technique
Make a loop in the rope and bend it opposite the direction the knot will point. Pass the loop around the rope and back over the two strands

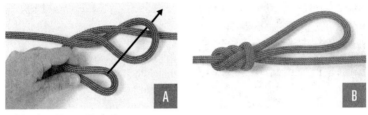

7.20 Inline Figure-Eight Loop

through the hole (photo 7.20.A). The loop strands and rope should be parallel as in the one-way square knot (photo 7.20.B). Dress and set the knot.

GARDA HITCH

This is a one-way, self-locking clutch that can be used for hauling a small pack up a cliff, particularly handy late in the day when you are tired. (If you will be hoisting heavy loads, however, it is not a substitute for a real pulley with a built-in cam.) It can also be used for improvising an ascending system in a self-rescue scenario or rigging a raising system for crevasse rescue—but practice this far in advance. Some have suggested it can be used for belaying a second on a climb. However, the knot won't release if climbers fall and are dangling.

Other Names
Alpine clutch
Ratchet knot
Guarde knot

Advantages
Fast and dirty ratcheting pulley.

Disadvantages
Nowhere near as efficient as a true ratcheting pulley for hauling loads, by an order of magnitude. Do not use this for heavy loads because of all the friction. May not work well with different-shaped or locking carabiners. It is best with oval carabiners, but few climbers carry these anymore. Can unclip itself in the blink of an eye if you are not paying attention.

Technique
Anchor a sling so that the bottom is about head height. Clip two offset-D carabiners to it with both gates facing down and out. (Using ovals, the

gates can face up and out to reduce the chance of unclipping.) Clip the rope through both carabiners (photo 7.21.A). Grab the strand that will not bear the load and push the clipped rope up toward the top of the carabiners (photo 7.21.B). Wrap the rope in hand around the back of both carabiners and clip it into the one nearer the load, outside to inside (photo 7.21.C). Try to keep the wraps around the spine when using the garda to avoid unclipping (photo 7.21.D).

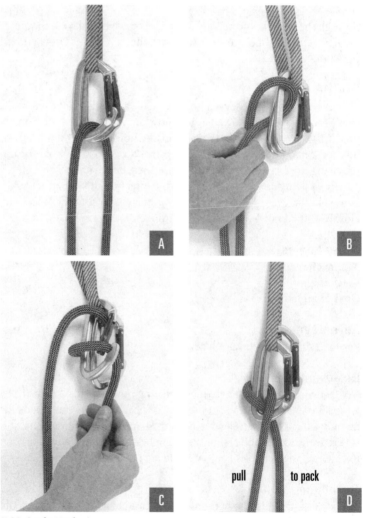

7.21 Garda Hitch

BOWLINE-ON-A-BIGHT

When setting up a two-bolt anchor, this knot is a fast way to equalize the load. Compared to a double butterfly, it takes a bit more futzing to get the tension right since each strand must be adjusted separately (it does not self-equalize). But the bowline-on-a-bight will not extend if one of the anchor points fails.

When rigging a cordelette anchor, sometimes the loop is not long enough to tie an overhand knot. A bowline-on-a-bight can allow for the necessary length and a solid anchor.

Other Names
Atomic clip

Advantages
Bombproof two-loop knot for anchors. No possibility of extension if there is an anchor failure. Less complicated to untie than a double butterfly.

Disadvantages
Adjusting the length of each loop is a minor nuisance.

Technique #1
Overhand: Make a bight in the rope that is twice as long as the desired eyes and tie a loose overhand loop. Reach through the loop with one hand (photo 7.22.A) and grab both strands of the rope just past the knot (photo 7.22.B). Flip the loop over your hand (photo 7.22.C) and pull the slack back

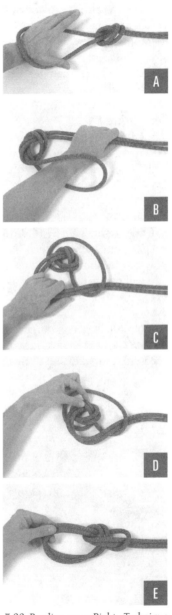

7.22 *Bowline-on-a-Bight, Technique #1, Overhand*

through the hole (photo 7.22.D) (photo 7.22.E).

The easiest way to adjust the bowline is to leave the knot loose. Feed extra rope into the knot and pull the associated loop out until it is the approximate size. Fine-tune the loop sizes by pinching all four strands where they cross to hold the hole open and pulling on the strand of the short loop where it emerges from the bight. Once it is adjusted, set the knot.

Technique #2

Passed Bow: Make a long bight in the rope and start to tie a single bowline using the hand-flick method (see Bowline, Chapter 6). Pass the bight around the rope as normal but do not go back through the hole. Instead, slip the bight over the two loops and flip it up past the knot.

Variations

Cordelette-on-a-Bight (Cordonbight): Clip the cordelette into the anchor points and equalize the bights as usual. Select one bight and draw it out about 2 feet (the other bights run through your fingers and will pull in shorter). Make a half hitch in the long bight and slip it over the two short ones; this holds the bights together and makes two eyes.

Now make a bight in the long loop and slip it halfway through the two eyes. Pass the remainder of the long loop over the two new bights, then flip it forward and draw tight (photo 7.23).

7.23 Cordelette-on-a-Bight

BOWLINE-ON-A-COIL

I have a certain nostalgic fondness for this knot since the bowline-on-a-coil and Goldline ropes are what I used when learning to climb. However, when the foggy memories clear, I recall what a miserable experience it was to fall with this knot around my waist.

Even so, it is still a knot worth knowing. Should you ever forget your harness, the day won't be ruined if you use the bowline-on-a-coil for seconding or top roping. It can also be used on a middle person on a rope if you need to keep a group together. And young whippersnappers can discover what is was like when 5.10 was hard (find some old EB rockshoes for the full effect).

Other Names
Masochist's tie-in
Coils of pain

Advantages
Teaches respect for elders.

Disadvantages
See Other Names.

Technique
Pull two full arm spans of rope through your hands and pinch that spot to your belly button. Wrap three or four coils around your waist.

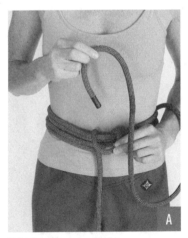

7.24 Bowline-on-a-Coil

If the tail is too short, just rotate all the coils to add more rope. Lay your hand across the standing part of the rope, palm down and thumb toward you, and rotate your wrist so that the palm is up to form a loop. Tuck this loop up underneath all the coils so it is sticking out the top above your belly button (photo 7.24.A). Now thread the end down through the loop, around the rope, and back up through the loop (photo 7.24.B). Pull everything snug, making sure the coils are tight around your waist (otherwise, the "swami" will ride up too high around your ribcage and suffocate you). Back up the knot with an overhand around the uppermost coil. Spew to other climbers about how tough you are (optional).

Chapter 8

Knots for Canoeing & Kayaking

In a way, this chapter is a cheat because many of the knots presented earlier have nautical origins. What remains are knots that are particularly well suited for use on and near the water.

TRUCKER'S HITCH

When I was a whitewater raft guide in the '70s, we used to pile a half dozen inflated 16-foot rafts on a trailer, put four more on the flatbed truck, and then barrel down the highway to keep our shuttles on time. To keep the rafts from flying, which occasionally happened when someone didn't do the job right, we used this simple block-and-tackle system, which was easy to reposition and secure.

The trucker's hitch is good to know, but one-inch solid webbing straps with heavy-duty, spring-loaded aluminum buckles sure make things easier.

Advantages

Great way to secure any bulky object on a car or trailer. Useful for strapping dunnage and equipment into a raft. The knot can be repositioned easily once the tension is released.

Disadvantages

Wears out ropes in a hurry unless the knot is repositioned or a carabiner used.

Technique

Anchor one end and pass the rope over the boats or whatever the load is. Make a bight in the rope a full arm's reach above the anchor on the other side and tie a figure-eight slip knot (photo 8.1.A) with the sliding part toward the end. Pass the tail through the anchor and back up through the slip knot's loop (photo 8.1.B). Pull hard on the tail to tighten the load down and quickly throw in a slip knot at the loop to hold the tension (photo 8.1.C). Pull the loop out and finish with several half hitches around the taut rope.

If you need more cranking power, pass the rope through the anchor and loop one more time. This will increase the pulley effect and tends to be self-binding due to friction.

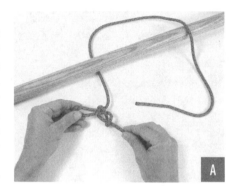

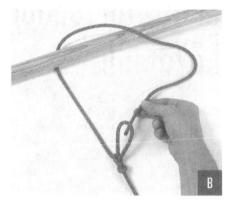

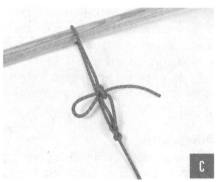

8.1 *Trucker's Hitch*

MOORING HITCH

As the name implies, this is a good knot for tying up a boat. But it is also a useful quick-release sliding knot anytime a line is under tension. After the rope has been passed around the anchor (often a tree or shrub onshore), the knot can be tied out in the open so you aren't crouched under branches. With a long tail, you can release the hitch from the dry comfort of your boat and still have a line to shore, which is sometimes handy when you are setting out into a current.

Advantages

Holds well yet releases with a good tug. If pulled tight and used with lighter loads, it acts like a releasable tautline hitch.

Disadvantages

May not grip well on some ropes; just slips up to the anchor but still releases.

Technique

Pass the rope around the anchor point. On the non–load-bearing strand, form a crossing loop with the tail on the underside (photo 8.2.A). Lay this loop over the load-bearing rope and pinch the two together at the bottom. Make a bight in the tail with your free hand. Feed the bight over the first strand, under the rope, and over the third strand (photo 8.2.B). Pull on the bight to draw everything up snug (photo 8.2.C). When it's time to go, just give the tail a sharp tug.

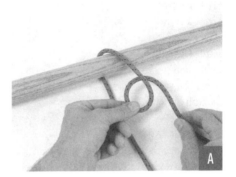

SLIP-FREE HITCH

8.2 Mooring Hitch

A fun knot that is great for tying up boats along the river. This clever arrangement of loops has the advantage that the rope is double backed around the anchor, so a knot or kink will not stop your escape. This modified version of the highwayman's hitch offers better security and quicker release.

Other Names
Draw hitch

Advantages
Less likely to get stuck, especially if your painter (bow or stern line) has a knot in it.

Disadvantages
"How does that go again? Show me one more time." "Okay, just once more." Instant release doesn't allow you to control your departure, so sometimes it is good to hold onto the painter after a knot has been released.

Technique
Make a bight in the rope and pass it behind the anchor point (photo 8.3.A). Bring another bight up from the rope and pass it over the first bight from the front (photo 8.3.B). Make a bight in the tail and slip it through the original bight (photo 8.3.C). Snug it all down (photo 8.3.D).

Do not pull the tail until you are sure you are ready to cast off!

BUNTLINE HITCH
When rigging safety lines on rafts, you don't want them coming undone. This is a good, low-bulk hitch for semipermanently anchoring a rope.

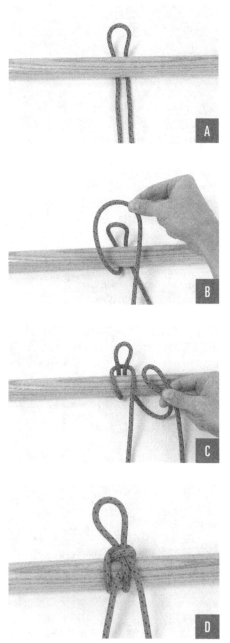

8.3 Slip-Free Hitch

Advantages

More secure than two half hitches. Unlikely to untie accidentally.

Disadvantages

Jams tight against the anchor point; sometimes has to be cut off.

Technique

Pass the rope around the anchor. Tie a clove hitch around the rope. Do this by passing the end under the rope and making one full wrap heading away from the anchor. Then bring the end up above the knot and make a full wrap around the rope with the tail going down through the loop (photo 8.4.A) (photo 8.4.B).

8.4 Buntline Hitch

SHEET BEND

A knot known to be at least 9,000 years old can't be all bad. Yet the sheet bend has earned a poor reputation because it is neither the strongest nor most secure knot for connecting ropes. The sheet bend has the same form as a bowline but is loaded on two of the four strands instead of three.

Other Names

Weaver's knot

Advantages

The fastest joining knot for ropes of similar diameter. Can be used to join two or three lines to a master line. Easily converted to a quick-release bend.

Disadvantages

Can fall apart when slack. Doesn't hold up well to repeated tugs.

Technique

Make a bight in whichever rope is stiffer. Slip the end of the other rope through the bight (photo 8.5.A). Wrap the end around both strands in the direction of the first rope's tail. Pass the end under its own rope (photo 8.5.B). Set the knot tight (photo 8.5.C).

If you need a fast disconnect, just pass a bight under at the last step.

Variation

Double Sheet Bend: When ropes of significantly different diameters are joined, or if they are particularly slippery, a normal sheet bend may not hold. Make a bight in the thicker rope and then tie a sheet bend and leave the knot loose. Just add one more wrap to the knot.

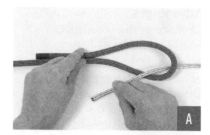
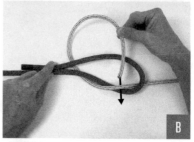

8.5 Sheet Bend

CLEAT HITCH

Cleats are common on sail and motor boats—and on docks, where canoeists and kayakers may want to tie up their craft. Other than specific-use applications, there is only one way to properly tie off a line to a cleat; anything else proves you are a landlubber.

Advantages

Quick way to fasten a line. The line can be released under load and controlled—this is where climbers get the term "belay."

Disadvantages

No quick release.

Technique

Bring the line to the ear of the cleat farthest from direction of pull. Make a complete wrap around the base of the cleat (photo 8.6.A).

Cross over the top diagonally, go under the ear, and then cross over the top in the other direction and under the ear to complete a figure eight (photo 8.6.B). Finish with a half hitch over the closer ear (photo 8.6.C); the tail should point away from where the line came in (photo 8.6.D).

To stow extra line on a mast cleat: Coil the excess line clockwise. Bring the coil close to the cleat, reach through with one hand to take some line leading from the cleat and twist a loop. Bring the loop through the coils and hang it over the ear of the cleat. Snug it so the coil won't fall off when the boat rolls.

PALOMAR KNOT
The palomar knot is among the easiest methods for attaching a fishhook to a line, especially for those with big clutzy fingers.

Advantages
Simple to tie, even with fine lines and small hooks. Works as well as many other fishhook knots without the hassle.

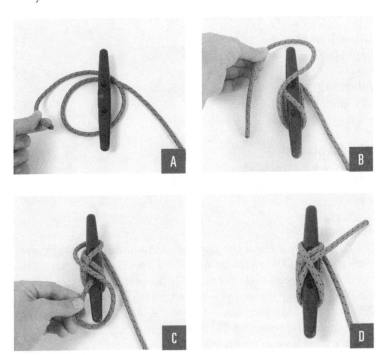

8.6 Cleat Hitch

Disadvantages
May not hold with very slippery line.

Technique
Pass a long bight through the eye. Then tie a loose overhand knot around the line and tail (photo 8.7.A). Slip the loop over the fishhook and then past the knot (photo 8.7.B). Lubricate the line with water, cinch it all up, and trim the tail (photo 8.7.C).

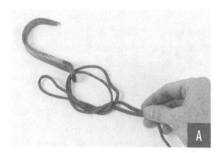

BLOOD KNOT
This simple bend is one of the strongest ways to repair a broken fishing line.

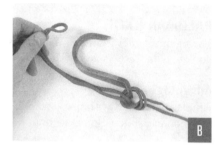

Other Names
Barrel knot

Advantages
Less complicated than other knots for fishing line.

Disadvantages
Doesn't work as well when joining lines of different diameters.

8.7 Palomar Knot

Technique
Overlap the two ends of the lines by several inches. Pinch them together at the middle and wrap one of the lines five times around the other. Bring the end back and tuck it between the two strands (photo 8.8.A). Then wrap the second line five times in the opposite direction. Bring the end back and tuck it next to the other end, pointed in the other direction (photo 8.8.B). Moisten the line and gently tighten, then trim the ends close to the knot (photo 8.8.C).

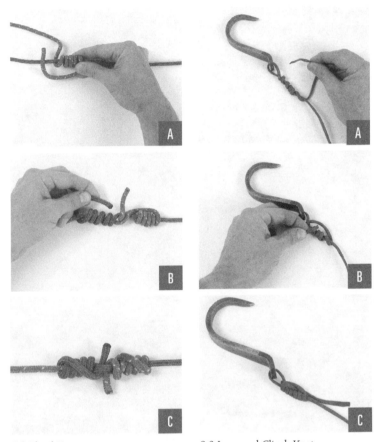

8.8 Blood Knot   8.9 Improved Clinch Knot

Variation

Improved Clinch Knot: Half of a blood knot tied to a hook is called a clinch knot. This works well but can be made to grab slippery line better by a slight modification. Slip the end through the eye, then make at least five wraps around the line going away from the hook. Bring the end back and slip it between the two strands next to the eye (photo 8.9.A). Pass the end through the loop just formed (photo 8.9.B) and cinch it all up (photo 8.9.C).

Glossary

Abrasion resistance: The amount of abuse a fiber or rope can endure from rubbing against other fibers (internal abrasion) or a surface (external abrasion).

Anchor point: A tree, rock horn, bolt hanger, piton, chock, camming device, cleat, shrub, or just about anything else you can use for attaching a rope. Some are better than others.

Belay: The verb means to secure a person with a rope; used as a noun, it's the spot where the climber stops and builds an anchor.

Belay device: By increasing friction or pinching the rope, these devices magnify the braking force of the hand.

Bend: When two rope ends are tied together. Many so-called "knots" are actually bends.

Bight: A tight fold in a rope.

Capsize: When a knot morphs into another knot. This happens with some but not all knots, depending upon which strands are pulled.

Cordage: Usually refers to small-diameter line; also can refer to thicker rope and webbing.

Cordelette: A large loop of accessory cord used by climbers for creating a multipoint anchor. It allows all the anchors to share the load such that, if one fails, the others will continue to hold.

Creep: When subjected to a sustained load, synthetic fibers permanently stretch due to cold flow and a rope elongates from compaction. Ropes that must be truly static are de-creeped by prestretching before use.

Dress: An important step in tying many knots. After all the turns and crossings are done, everything must be tidied up to achieve full strength. Crossed strands can significantly weaken the knot.

Dynamic load: A force placed on a rope in a very short time frame, such as when a climber falls. High-elongation ropes spread out the duration of impact, giving a softer catch.

Dynamic rope: A rope made of nylon and constructed so that it will stretch to absorb the forces of a sudden impact.

Energy absorption: The more a rope stretches, the more energy it can absorb from elongation of yarns and friction of fibers moving against one another. After stopping hard falls, so much heat is produced that fibers melt together.

Fall factor: This is the length of the fall divided by the amount of rope that absorbs the impact. Most climbing falls are under factor 0.5 while the ropes are tested with a factor 1.7 drop (2.0 is the maximum).

Fatigue: While external abrasion is obvious, internal wear and tear can weaken ropes without hints. All the small impacts can add up and greatly reduce a rope's performance; this is called rope fatigue.

Fiber: Made of natural or synthetic material, this is the smallest component of a rope or webbing.

Flake: Each loop in a coil is called a flake. To flake a rope is to remove one coil at a time.

Frapping turns: The wraps that go around lashings to bind them tight.

Friction hitch: A runner attached to a rope that grabs when weighted, and slides when tension is released.

Hank: A tight coil of cord with frapping turns around the center. Also called a skein.

Heat resistance: Some synthetic fibers lose half their strength well below their melting point. Natural fibers and aramids will burn, rather than melt, at higher temperatures than many other synthetics.

Heat set: A step in the production of a dynamic rope that maximizes elasticity by heating the nylon under controlled conditions.

Hitch: A knot that attaches a rope to an object, including another rope.

Hockle: A permanent bump in laid ropes, usually with significant strength loss. Hockles form when the rope is loaded before kinks have been removed.

Impact force: This is the amount of force experienced by a falling climber and his or her last piece of protection. The amount of force depends upon the fall factor, not the distance of the fall.

Kernmantle: A rope made with a core (*kern*) of twisted strands that is covered by a tightly braided sheath (*mantle*).

Kink: An annoying sharp bend in a rope caused by twisting forces.

Kilonewton (kN): A unit of force. 1 kN equals 102 kilograms (kg) equals 225 pounds of force (lbf).

Laid: A form of rope construction made by twisting rather than braiding fibers. This usually refers to three strands twisted together; each strand is made of three twisted fiber bundles.

Loop: Give a bight a half twist so the strands cross; this forms a loop. Also called a crossing turn.

Low-elongation rope: A rope, generally made of nylon and/or polyester, that is designed to have minimal stretch under body weight and moderate stretch when forces are greater. Commonly used for caving, hauling heavy loads, and top-rope climbing.

Prusik: A knot made with a loop of cord used to ascend a rope; the cord itself is often called a "Prusik sling." When ascending a rope using any knot, many call it "prusiking." If any mechanical ascender is used, the person is "jumaring" (named after an ascender) or "jugging" (jargon).

Rack: Loops of webbing or accessory cord are prone to tangling or snagging, so climbers reduce them into smaller packages called racks. A rack is also an arrangement or a grouping of any gear used for climbing.

Round turn: A full wrap around an object, making one and a half circles, so both ends point in the same direction.

Runner: A loop of webbing; commonly used by climbers. The loop is created either with a knot or a commercial sewing machine.

Safety factor: The ratio between the breaking strength to the working load limit of a system. When human life is involved, a ratio of at least 5 is recommended and 15 is common in rescue and industrial applications. For example, if a carabiner is rated at 23 kilonewtons (kN), it should not be used with loads greater than 4.6 kN (1,034 pounds/force or "lbf").

Set: After the knot has been dressed, it needs to be drawn up tight so that is properly formed, to "set" the knot. Setting a knot ensures that it will perform in a predictable manner.

Sheath: A hollow braid that surrounds and protects the rope's core.

Skein: A coil of rope that is formed around a wheel, stick, or other object that is then removed.

Sling: See runner.

Spill: When a knot comes untied, sometimes intentionally, sometimes not.

Stacking: Pulling an end away from a coil of rope usually results in tangles. To prevent this, the rope is uncoiled (stacked) into a heap on the ground.

Static rope: Ropes that have almost no stretch. These are not used for most outdoor applications, except sailing, because they cannot absorb any impact force.

Stopper knot: A knot tied in the end of the rope to prevent an accident such as a climber rappelling off the end or the rope slipping through a block and tackle.

Tail: The leftover rope end dangling from one side of a knot.

Top roping: A form of practice climbing during which the climber is held from a rope above. This usually refers to a setup with an anchor at the top of the cliff and a belayer at the bottom (sometimes called a "slingshot belay").

Turn: A half wrap around an object.

UIAA: The *Union Internationale des Associations d'Alpinisme* is a world-wide coalition of national climbing clubs that sets standards for climbing equipment. The CEN (*Comité Européen de Normalisation*) uses the same tests.

Webbing: Flat tape, made of natural or synthetic fibers, that is either solid or tubular.

Working load limit (WLL): The maximum load that should be applied to a piece of equipment as determined by the Safety Factor.

Yarn: The result of twisting fibers together. An early step in the production of rope or fabric.

Index

ABOUT THE AUTHOR

Clyde Soles has been tying knots in the outdoors for about four decades. He is a Colorado-based freelance writer and photographer with a passion for adventure and travel.

Clyde earned a B.A. in Nature Photojournalism from the University of Colorado in Boulder and worked on his M.S. at the Brooks Institute of Photography in Santa Barbara, California. He was an editor at *Rock & Ice* magazine for seven years and the founder of *Trail Runner* magazine. Currently, he is a Senior Contributing Editor for *GearTrends* magazine, and his articles and photographs have been published in many other publications.

His previous titles for The Mountaineers Books are *Rock & Ice Gear: Equipment for the Vertical World* (2000), *Climbing: Training for Peak Performance* (2002), and *Climbing: Expedition Planning* (2003).

THE MOUNTAINEERS, founded in 1906, is a nonprofit outdoor activity and conservation club, whose mission is "to explore, study, preserve, and enjoy the natural beauty of the outdoors . . . . " Based in Seattle, Washington, the club is now the third-largest such organization in the United States, with seven branches throughout Washington State.

The Mountaineers sponsors both classes and year-round outdoor activities in the Pacific Northwest, which include hiking, mountain climbing, ski-touring, snowshoeing, bicycling, camping, kayaking and canoeing, nature study, sailing, and adventure travel. The club's conservation division supports environmental causes through educational activities, sponsoring legislation, and presenting informational programs. All club activities are led by skilled, experienced volunteers, who are dedicated to promoting safe and responsible enjoyment and preservation of the outdoors.

If you would like to participate in these organized outdoor activities or the club's programs, consider a membership in The Mountaineers. For information and an application, write or call The Mountaineers, Club Headquarters, 300 Third Avenue West, Seattle, Washington 98119; 206-284-6310.

The Mountaineers Books, an active, nonprofit publishing program of the club, produces guidebooks, instructional texts, historical works, natural history guides, and works on environmental conservation. All books produced by The Mountaineers fulfill the club's mission.

Send or call for our catalog of more than 450 outdoor titles:

The Mountaineers Books
1001 SW Klickitat Way, Suite 201
Seattle, WA 98134
800-553-4453
mbooks@mountaineersbooks.org
www.mountaineersbooks.org

 Leave No Trace strives to educate visitors about the nature of their recreational impacts, as well as offer techniques to prevent and minimize such impacts. Leave No Trace is best understood as an educational and ethical program, not as a set of rules and regulations.

For more information, visit *www.LNT.org*, or call 800-332-4100.

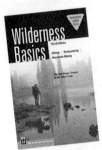

ALSO IN THE MOUNTAINEERS OUTDOOR BASICS SERIES

Wilderness Basics, *San Diego chapter of The Sierra Club*
A classic handbook for the outdoor novice interested in hiking, backpacking, paddling, and mountain biking.

OTHER TITLES YOU MIGHT ENJOY FROM THE MOUNTAINEERS BOOKS

Day Hiker's Handbook: Get Started with the Experts, *Mike Lanza*
Learn how to get started, what gear to choose, and how to handle possible dangers

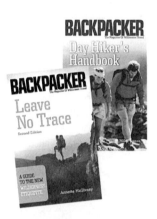

Leave No Trace: A Guide to the New Wilderness Ethic,
Annette McGivney
Learn how to minimize your impact on the environment and support the LNT Center for Outdoor Ethics

Don't Forget the Duct Tape: Tips and Tricks for Emergency Gear Repair, *Kristin Hostetter*
Pack this little guide with you and be an outdoor fixit guru!

Staying Found: The Complete Map & Compass Handbook,
June Fleming
An easy-to-understand handbook for learning map and compass

Everyday Wisdom: 1001 Expert Tips for Hikers,
Karen Berger
Expert tips and tricks for hikers and backpackers selected from one of the most popular *Backpacker* magazine columns

THE MOUNTAINEERS BOOKS